A Heroine in Heels

Ardre Orie

A Heroine in Heels

Copyright © 2015 by 13th & Joan Publishing

All rights reserved. No part of this book may be reproduced or transmitted in any form or by any means without written permission of the author.

ISBN 978-0-9916015-3-0

Acknowledgements

Nothing monumental can be achieved in isolation. A heartfelt expression of gratitude to all of the amazing people that helped to make this book a success:

Photography Team

Lead Photographer:

Charlton Hudnell, My Miracle Moments Photography
www.mymiraclemoments.com

Contributing Photographers:

Abhik Kar (AK Photography)
www.facebook.com/akarphotography

Amy Kostoryz

Jirad
www.jirard.com

Megan Dougherty
www.megansimage.com

Shaina Leigh Photography
www.shainaleighphotography.com

Makeup

Creative Director of Makeup Artistry:

Perris "Sebastian" Hull

I Love Me
www.ilovemeglam.com
www.ilovemeorganics.com

Contributing Glam Squad Members

Alex D. Holliman, Designer
Katie Brinson, Wardrobe Stylist
Tova Treadwell, Wardrobe Stylist
Wynton Harris, Hair Care Specialist
LaCreasia Marcus, Nail Care Specialist
LeGair Luxury Brand
Van Miller International Fashion House

Dedication

To my beloveds Lauren & London. Never forget that you already have all the power that you will ever need. It lies within.

Table of Contents

Foreword 1
Introduction 7

1   Love featuring Bianca Wilfork 11
2   Pain featuring Arthlene LeGair 21
3   Hope featuring Alima Albari 33
4   Fear featuring Arnita Jackson 41
5   Envy featuring Koereyelle DuBose 49
6   Pride featuring Raven Clements Thomas 61
7   Courage featuring Dar'Shun Kendrick 69
8   Anger featuring Jill Tracey 79
9   Fatigue featuring Vanessa Henderson 89
10 Insecurity featuring Elizabeth Clark 99
11 Sadness featuring Yvonne Fry 111
12 Joy featuring Gwynnis Mosby 121
13 Grace featuring Monica Wright 133
14 Desire featuring Lovilla Santiago 141

Conclusion 151
Endnotes 157
Lead Photographer 159
Creative Director of Makeup Artistry 161
About the Author 163

Foreword

Every woman is or will be a heroine at some point in her life. The troubles of the world often leave us with indescribable strength, courage, and the will to save ourselves. For some, this sentiment is at specific moments in life, and then there are those whose cape is a part of their everyday attire. Those are the women that you see or listen to and become further intrigued. They are the women who are willing to give the very essence of who they are to help those in need, change the world around them, and leave a lasting legacy. I refer to each of these women as a heroines in heels.

her·o·ine
ˈherō-in/
noun
singular: heroine; plural: heroines
"A woman admired or idealized for her courage, outstanding achievements, or noble qualities."[1]

Inevitably, when discussing heroism, the word "power" abounds. As the mother of two daughters and a life-long feminist, it is imperative that I do everything in my power to ensure that women and girls understand their value and the power that lies within.

The word "power" is used so freely because it is my belief that it is just that available if we learn how to channel it. It is my belief that power circulates through us just as blood and oxygen and that it is replenished continually. I believe that power is infinite as long as we are aware of how to most effectively utilize it. To this end, I believe that women and girls possess a tremendous amount of power that is not often recognized in lieu of the many contrived messages imposed by society. Additionally, we lack the filter to sift through messages provided to us through entertainment versus those that should build the foundational evidence for what a life filled with heroism is and should be.

The problem with all of this is that little girls are watching. If we lie dormant and do nothing, we will, in turn, have forward generations of women who are not cultivated to recognize signs of heroism and purposeful living as well as those who place the greatest emphasis on the utilization of outward appearance to leverage a false level of power.

Power is defined as the ability to do something or act in a particular way, especially as a faculty or quality. Every person needs power. Every person needs the ability to overcome life's obstacles as they are as certain as the wind that blows. The world would have us believe that our power can only be leveraged from the use of our bodies and ability to be hypersexualized through imagery.

In an effort to address this scenario, I penned an open letter to let young ladies know that there are options. We don't have to resort to the antiquated female stereotypes like the sex kitten, damsel in distress, or the victim to harness our power. If we truly put things into perspective, we will still be responsible for saving ourselves in the end. Here is the letter that I wrote a few years back:

Open Letter to All of the Little Girls Watching:

Dear Girls,

Let me first start by saying that I am not writing this letter to throw hate or shade. I believe every woman to be beautiful in her own right. I am writing this letter to simply present the case that, in all things, we have options.

This morning I woke up and began to read the news and engage in social media as I often do. Before 10 a.m., I saw two pictures of two women, who I consider beautiful creatures and very much influencers in today's society, which encouraged me to write this letter to you.

The first photograph was a swimsuit-clad Kim Kardashian. Kim was "giving life" and showing that motherhood is a beautiful thing. After having a baby and taking a great deal of heat from the mainstream media about her weight, I believe that she deserves to have a moment of glory to bask in the fact that she still looks amazing. If you ask me, every new mother deserves this opportunity. Here is an example of where you have options. In the event you wish to celebrate your body, you don't really need an audience to do so. If you feel the need to share with others, you still have an option to wear something that looks amazing but doesn't reveal all of your glory to the world. You have options. The ability to wear swimwear and feel good about ourselves is a celebration alone in a world that tells us that we have to be perfect. It is your option as to how you share these moments. Am I saying that ladies should not post pictures of themselves at the beach or poolside? No. I am simply saying that you have options.

The second photograph that grabbed the media's attention was Nikki Minaj, in true Barbie doll fashion, giving fierce face and more than a handful of cleavage.

In my opinion, Nikki is one of the illest businesswomen in the game right now. She has taken control of her business and brand.

As an entrepreneur, I can only salute her. Whether Nikki reveals her chest or not, she will still be a powerful force in the music industry and any other business endeavor that she touches. If you aspire to rise to the top of a male-dominated field, such as rap or any STEM (science, technology, engineering, and mathematics) field, you have options as to how to get there. You don't have to be naked to be your best.

It is without question that pictures such as these get mad love, but I have to ask: What is mainstream media teaching our girls about their value? Does it lie in their ability to be naked? Do you only get more likes, fans, followers, love when you show more skin? Consider the little girl who posted her first selfie on Instagram or Facebook and is fully clothed; has society taught us that this means that she is not "turned up" enough? Is she worth less in today's society?

I know that comparing celebrities to everyday superstars is like comparing apples to oranges, but I still believe the point to be valid. Celebrities are at a heightened level of attention as they capture our hearts, minds, and spirits with their music and contributions to the arts, but I also want little girls watching to know that *it is okay to keep your clothes on*. It's okay if you don't earn the award for best twerker in your school. It is and should be normal to aspire to earn the highest grades and not the highest number of followers. *The pursuit of your dreams has absolutely nothing to do with your ability to show your skin and everything to do with your willingness to work hard for it.* I am not saying that the ladies above are not hard workers, because that is clearly not the case. I am simply saying that *this is not the only way.*

Just know that things are not always what they seem. There are many ways to the top and you have to be certain to choose the one that will make you the most happy and that will allow you to be true to who you really are, not who the world says you should be.

As an adult, I have the option to filter the things that I want to receive in my spirit and into my life. As I continue to come of age, I have a much better understanding of how I want the world to see me. You don't have that choice. You are still very impressionable, which is why I was so compelled to write this letter.

I write this letter in tears, because I so desperately want women and girls to know that, even though the media is only obsessed with you when you take your clothes off or do things that don't speak to your brain power, this is not the true determination of your worth. You, with all your clothes on and all of your flaws, all of your heartbreak, triumph, and ambitions, are enough. I know you are watching the messages that the world is sending you, but believe me when I say you are enough!

Just remember love and light will find you, not because you took off your clothes but because you loved yourself first. Keep believing in yourself and, as I always say, stay turned up to follow your dreams. Never forget, in all things, you have options.

In the early twentieth century, the American ideals of beauty began to shift to an influence of celebrities and those featured in feature films. Prior to this time, societal class as well as leadership, power, and status shaped culture as we knew it.

I can only wonder: Did this shift influence our ideals about heroism as well?

Today, media would have us believe that heroism is attained by many superficial suitors who have no real essence or plight to make the world a better place. Society has taught women to idolize celebrities and many who have acquired popularity on social media through endless selfies and countless alterations to their bodies. Society has taught women to idolize women who use their bodies to further their personal mission.

There is without question an underrepresentation of women idolized for their daily heroic, selfless acts of courage. Caring for families, excelling in school, fearlessly rising to the top as executives in otherwise male-dominated fields, maintaining multiple jobs, leading the charge in entrepreneurship—women fight each day to make the world a better place. As I have grown up, I have witnessed an overwhelming assortment of women and girls depicted as princesses or damsels in distress. It is my personal mission to bring attention to the ladies who recognize their inner power and act, serve, and live as heroines. This book is one of many attempts to garner a higher platform to reach the hearts and minds of women and girls of all ages to counter the images that society has imposed. This book is purposed to recognize a heroine in heels and further resolve that she lives inside each of us.

Introduction

Women have long been portrayed as victims, the weaker species, the damsel in distress. Society has given us so many messages about our roles that we are often led to believe that we are limited in our capabilities. There is nothing further from the truth as countless women defy the odds, breakthrough barriers, and unleash power that can often only be explained by the supernatural.

The greatest challenge of life lies in our ability to consciously harness heroine power in our daily lives and to know without question that we have been gifted with this power. It lies within us, runs through our veins, and fuels our souls. The question of our existence becomes: What must I know or be able to do to allow infinite power to manifest in my daily walk?

Just as we decide which shoe to wear with each ensemble, we should place a great deal of emphasis on deciding which strategy to use to maneuver the thoughts that guide our hearts and minds during life's obstacles and successes.

Although there are countless women harnessing their power and executing heroic feats daily, there are too many examples that mimic the disparity between the actual versus realized value of women in the workplace, society, and the world.

The "Women's Leadership Gap" written by the Center for American Progress reports the following alarming statistics:

Although women hold almost 52 percent of all professional-level jobs, American women lag substantially behind men when it comes to their representation in leadership positions:

- They are only 14.6 percent of executive officers, 8.1 percent of top earners, and 4.6 percent of Fortune 500 CEOs.
- In the financial services industry, they make up 54.2 percent of the labor force, but are only 12.4 percent of executive officers, and 18.3 percent of board directors. None are CEOs.
- They account for 78.4 percent of the labor force in health care and social assistance but only 14.6 percent of executive officers and 12.4 percent of board directors. None, again, are CEOs.
- In the legal field, they are 45.4 percent of associates—but only 25 percent of nonequity partners and 15 percent of equity partners.
- In medicine, they comprise 34.3 percent of all physicians and surgeons but only 15.9 percent of medical school deans.
- In information technology, they hold only 9 percent of management positions and account for only 14 percent of senior management positions at Silicon Valley startups.[2]

We must continue to reveal the truth about the power, capabilities, and qualifications of women so that the damsel in distress becomes a myth and a heroine in heels becomes the affirmable truth.

Within every great story of heroism, there are associated key elements. Life teaches us that we must expect these elements to not only take place in our lives but also to shape it.

Just as we would select a pair of heels to complete an ensemble, we must learn to seek the power in the selection of a thought process or energy from which to channel as we embark upon life's daily tests and journeys.

What we know to be certain of humans is that their emotions are abundant. Emotions control us; we are governed by them. Whether times are good or tumultuous, our emotions lead the way. If we examine the manifestation of our emotions in our lives, we could deepen our understanding of how to make them work for our benefit and prosperity.

Every amazing story featured in this book is purposed to demonstrate the correlation between the power and energy that resides within each emotion and the construction of strategies which we must find refuge in using to channel our greatest power and potential. All of the power that we will ever need, we already possess.

CHAPTER I

Love

Love

ləv/
noun
"An intense feeling of deep affection."³

> *Love is the imprint stamped on the walls of our souls.*
> —Ardre Orie

My absolute favorite writings on love are found in the Bible.

> Love is patient, love is kind. It does not envy, it does not boast, it is not proud. It does not dishonor others, it is not self-seeking, it is not easily angered, it keeps no record of wrongs. Love does not delight in evil but rejoices with the truth. It always protects, always trusts, always hopes, always perseveres. (1 Corinthians 13:4–7, New International Version)

This beautiful scripture embodies what true love is. Anything outside of this definition is another sentiment, not love.

It has become apparent to me that whether the action results in a positive or negative outcome, love is the often mysterious motivator behind most of our actions.

I believe that we are programmed to align with love, and from this emotion, we are either empowered or victimized.

I found true love at the age of fourteen, although I was too immature, broken, and bound to recognize it. Still riding the frequency of "powerful single women not in need of a man syndrome," I thought I'd humor myself, because that's what girls in high school do, date, right?

To my surprise, this young man was seemingly different from the rest. He had a level of maturity that I had not encountered. We were both shocked when we discovered that we were in love. You know the puppy love kind. I would venture to say that we could have imagined our lives together in the future.

My mother adored him. We spent countless hours together such that he taught me to drive. He treated me with so much care that many of our friends would deem our relationship to be a match made in heaven.

Because I had no point of reference for love, I would eventually self-destruct.

Our puppy love would span for a total of six years. We were absolute best friends, and he was closer than many family members. We grew up together and bonded as if we had known each other our entire lives. When it ended, I had no remorse. It was as if he had never existed. I was just that coldhearted.

I would later learn that my "Queen of Ice" disposition was a cowardly coping mechanism that I had used for so many years to shield myself from the hurt and impact that the loss of relationships and people could have in my life. Had I known love, I would have clung to him and held tightly. Had I recognized love for its true value, I would have never interchanged it with the notion that it was dispensable. Had I known love, I would have understood the magnitude of its immeasurable value. Had I known love, I would have given it in return, for it is the greatest gift that we can share and unwrap.

As life progressed, I returned to my non-believer sentiments on love and lived in a self-destructive and sarcastic state of mind focusing my attention towards attaining success in college. I could guarantee and control my success in this arena, because the outcome was a direct result of my actions. Love doesn't allow us to control it. It just occurs. This is the reason that it so often frightens us. It is quite possible to love and lose. Why would anyone risk everything for a possible failure?

In my mind, this strategy or imaginary feeling was neither smart nor strategic and lacked wit.

I later realized that I had not only given up on love, but I had also lost my hope in people. I believed people to be dispensable, although there were many whom I valued immensely. This empty nest in my heart would cause me to question the need to give, receive, and replenish love in our lives. Were we really all placed here to covet and not share or receive love? The most glaring reveal was that I never believed that I deserved to be loved, so I didn't.

Four years later, God granted me a do-over. He reinstated my overdrawn bank account and allowed me to rediscover the same love that I had allowed to slip through my hands like grains of sand. My high school sweetheart asked me to be his wife, and, without hesitation, I obliged.

Not only did God grant me love, but He also granted abundance: Our union was solidified by three amazing children who teach us daily how to be better human beings and how to love.

Now I understand that love does not have to be forced. It just is. Just as we exist, love exists, and we get to decide where we will place such badges of honor.

After being granted what I feel is an overabundance through marriage and motherhood, I place love badges in as many locations as I can. I now recognize that the more love we give, the more our love is replenished. Even when we feel that we have lost, we have only gained, because love simply cannot be lost, only replenished. We must recognize that we are deserving of it and, most importantly, qualified to share it with others.

When we love ourselves, our worth is increased; thus, we have the power to love others and change the world. Love is power.

No Longer Anonymous

I recognize you in the darkness. I can hear your smile. You warm me like the sunlight every once in a while. I can hear you in the distance and I now know you by name. There is not one who is sweeter or one who moves me quite the same. I ran from your embrace for far, far too long, and now that I am no longer afraid, I want to listen to your song.

Your lyrics bring me peace and your melodies soothe my soul. Your glory is for the world to behold.

I recognize you in the darkness. I can hear you smile. You warm me like the sunlight every once in a while. I can hear you in the distance and I now know you by name. *Love.* There is not one who is sweeter or one who moves me quite the same.

A Heroine in Heels: Bianca Wilfork

In a time where short-lived, high-profile relationships are glorified and divorce is the norm, emerges a hero that would teach those smart enough to pay close attention the strength that radiates from true love.

Society continues to teach us that women who center their lives on their families are weak. I remember being ridiculed at work for choosing to spend more time with my family. Not as much now that I am older, but I would often hear people say, "You don't have to do everything together," in reference to my family and our stick-together attitude. I had a boss that once uttered, "They will get along just fine without you." This could not have been true, because it would also mean that the contributions that I was so happy to make to my family were of no value.

Although mainstream media does not give us many examples of marriages that stand the test of time and families that make it work by any means necessary, I and those smart enough to pay close attention get to be influenced by Bianca Wilfork. Bianca Wilfork lives her life for her family. As the wife of celebrated NFL Defensive Tackle Vince Wilfork, she leaves no question what team she plays on.

My memories of B, as I affectionately call her, go back as far as I can remember into my adolescence. She was a close friend during our formative stages. She was the girl that was cool with everyone leaving very little room for negative energy. She was always upbeat and had a spark that could make anyone laugh. In retrospect, the emerging theme of her character is loyalty. She was always a loyal friend, and that still remains true today. After publishing my first book, she called to wish me well but also purchased several copies and told the world that she supported my work. This is who she is today but also who she has always been.

Today, she is the epitome of a wife, mother, and unselfish love.

She can be seen proudly adorning herself and her family with custom sports jerseys, shoes, and anything else that she can find bearing the name Wilfork. She proudly represents for herself and her family. In a time where so many are focused on building brands, her brand is her family. While many spend time perfecting selfies to post on their social media accounts, her social media accounts are filled with images that demonstrate without question her love for her family.

And now, even though we live on two opposite ends of the country, we share the same love for the family structure. I had not recognized love when it was given to me and fumbled my way toward opening my heart.

What had Bianca learned during the wonder years about love and relationships that allowed her to give of herself so fearlessly now?

Who had been the light that showed her how to love?

I would later learn that Bianca felt her best teachings about love came from the evolution of love in her life. Bianca spent much of her childhood as a nurturer. She notes that she was "not the girl who played with Barbies." She was the oldest of her siblings and often responsible for their well being. She often felt like the parent. This was Bianca's first living truth that love would often manifest in placing the lives of others before your own. Her embodiment of this can easily be recognized today. She is selfless with her love for her family and treasured friends. This would also easily explain why Bianca is able to love free from fear. She recognizes the power of love and how it can change the lives of those around her in a propitious way.

Although Bianca did not always dream of love, marriage, and the perfect family, her will to be happy manifested in a love that would bring happiness to her life. It is imperative to acknowledge that Bianca attributes the love for herself as a contributor to her life. Bianca loves without limits and gives freely of herself, but she also takes great pride in loving herself. Far too often, women mistake one action for the other or lack balance. It is imperative to seek, acknowledge, and stand in the opulence of self-love to in turn be positioned to share love with others. Love replenishes.

The family structure is the pinnacle of love. Love is the climax of life.

If we are able to conquer our trepidation and love fearlessly, we unlock the infinite power that creates a legacy.

When asked what she wanted her legacy to be, Bianca replied, "At the end of the day, I feel like I have already written my legacy. Anytime someone comes to me and says that I made a difference in their life, my mission is complete."

The exchange of love for each family member, allows each person to go out and circulate more love, infecting every other person touched. As people are infected, more positive energy circulates, and, in turn, we vibrate at our highest levels because we are secure in who we are, supported, and not afraid to fall, for love is the safety net. To love is to leave a legacy. To leave a legacy is to ignite power. The Wilforks will continue to circulate power, because they understand that love conquers all.

Bianca Farinas Wilfork

God has final say over all things, but I control the power I allow others to have in my life. I am my number-one motivation, and everything that I create is for my marriage and my family.

CHAPTER 2

Pain

Pain
pān/
noun
"Physical suffering or discomfort caused by illness or injury."[4]

Pain is the essence of passion.
—Ardre Orie

Often, pain is built from layers of life's experiences. Pain can be compared to a pomegranate. The outward appearance has no bearing on what lies within. When opened, there are several pockets of life's experiences, little moments of hurt, and they are not easily attained. The world teaches us to mask our pain because the revelation of it makes us weak. This is a lie. Time and experience has taught me that if we learn to acknowledge, address, and take action against the pain that life has caused us, we find the most hidden treasure: purpose. Like everyone else, my pain resides in layers, and I could write for days about the things that have caused me pain. The childhood friend that called me "black" as in not beautiful, the loss of friends, the struggle to discover and be proud of my true self, and the list goes on and on, but there are two layers that I regard as the most painful in my life. I am sharing them because I have learned that to acknowledge, address, and take action against my pain is an act of heroism. The three A's, as I refer to them, are what I have created as the basis for my "I AM" coaching system that I will one day share with the world. In the meantime, let's dive in.

Layer #1

Both pain and passion can evoke purpose. The greatest pain that I have ever experienced was self-inflicted. We can always find a way to insist that the circumstances that unfold in our lives cause us great pain and they often do. There is, however, no greater piercing sensation than the act of holding ourselves hostage and accountable for many of our life's events. As I share often, my source of pain was the absence of a male presence while growing up. I believed that it was my fault. I believed that I was unworthy of love. I believed that no man would see me as deserving of his love and affection if the one from which my soul was derived felt so. All lies.

As a coping mechanism, I numbed my heart. For so many years, I publicly discounted love. I denounced it. I projected fake strength to profess to the world that I was a strong woman who never really needed a man. Independence was the new black, and I wore it like a pair of stilettos. I had convinced myself of this false reality to the extent which I imagined my life with children but no husband. Can you say "destruction"?

This self-destructive pattern of thought remains popular now. It can be seen in our everyday lives, and, as the product of a single-parent home, I have absolute reverence and respect for the single mom. Furthermore, I acknowledge that this is not about blame. Relationships fail. Additionally, I am not speaking about scenarios in which one parent is fighting for the country or working in another city to provide or a parent who has passed away. In this instance, I am only speaking of absenteeism by choice. No matter how we desensitize our psyche to this notion, children were never meant to be raised alone. I watched my mother toil, work several jobs, and overcompensate emotionally to ensure that I never lacked from any end of the spectrum—and I didn't. My mother did such an amazing job that I truly believed that a man was not necessary. I thought that you only called them to fix things that you had no knowledge of fixing, such as vehicles, sinks, and heating systems. I had no earthly idea that men served other purposes. I watched as my grandmother toiled in the absence of a man, and I watched her manage her bills with pride and dignity, ensuring she never missed a payment. She cooked and cleaned and provided for her family in a major way. We never missed a meal, we never lacked clothing, and we were happy. So I thought.

A relationship with another person is actually a mirror. The ways in which you give and receive love are windows that peek into your soul. They reveal your pain. I was never good at giving love, because it caused me too much pain. I loved my friends, but I always kept a barrier on hand just in case I needed to build a wall. I did so with ease. I could end a friendship and feel absolutely nothing. I never purposely hurt anyone and tried to always be a source of comfort for my friends, which is why most are still great friends today; however, I learned that I, as well as my mother, grandmother and many others, masked great pain.

This self-inflicted pain could never be healed until I was forced to deal with the source of my pain and my truth and take ownership of all of the things that I had done to imprison my broken spirit.

I had not loved myself because I allowed someone else's feelings about me affect my own feelings about me. I had not loved myself enough, because I thought that loving someone meant that eventually they would leave as my father had done, so allowing that type of vulnerability was never a good idea.

The main point here is that this voice was not my own. I could not possibly be responsible for the choices of others. I had no influence on the decisions that were made. The world is filled with children like me who are hurting because they experienced detachment in the midst of a human's most vulnerable state: childhood. The pain is immense. There are few things that hurt your core like adopting detachment as a coping mechanism for pain. At no point in life should we under any circumstances allow another person to have such a tremendous impact on our perception of self. The only result is pain. We will always return void when we allow the voice of others to become our own. In this false truth, we will always inflict the greatest pain that we have ever known.

What I didn't realize was that, had I taken a chance to bite the seed of the pomegranate, I would have experienced its amazing juice. If the seed of the pomegranate is pain, then the juice of the pomegranate is the reward that we get to experience when we acknowledge, address, and take action against pain. The result for me would have been deeper relationships with friends and family and the ability to recognize true love when it was staring me in the face. As opposed to allowing this pain to encapsulate me, I decided to take action. The first step was that I began to listen to wise counsel. My mother spoke to me in great detail on several occasions about how to select a mate and how to discover love. She spoke from the "had I known then what I know now" stance. A heroine recognizes wise council and sits at her feet for wisdom and guidance. I set my heart on giving love and being loved. I determined that I wanted to be married and create a legacy. I resolved that I would do everything in my power to keep my family together in a healthy way. I would break the chain of bondage that had bound two generations of women in my family. I would become vulnerable to love and not pain. I would show my daughters what a loving marriage should look like so that they would have a point of reference. I would sip the pomegranate juice.

Layer #2

To experience love and loss is to live. When life slips through your hands, you wander seamlessly about with no rhyme or reason until your heart recognizes that love is and always will be a source of direction.

I received a text message while at work from my sorority sister Dazi, and it read, "Line Emergency." A "line" consists of the ladies who pledged at the exact time as you. You spend countless days and nights together to ensure that the business of the chapter is carried out. You bond immensely and become absolute family. Nadine was the youngest of the bunch and the life of the party. We nicknamed her Baby Pearl. We all felt a sense of responsibility for her. The last conversation that she and I had was when I picked her up and we drove to an event for our alma mater's homecoming. She began to cry in the car and express her admiration for me. In true motherly fashion, I told her to dry her eyes and that we absolutely could not ruin our makeup to indulge in another sappy moment that we'd always treasured together. That was the last time that I would see her face; it was the last time that we would cry together.

When I called Dazi back, she told me that Nadine had suddenly passed away. In complete disbelief, I told her to never call my place of work with untruths. I think that I hung up the phone. I sat in my office in total shock and disbelief. I transitioned into nonbelief. I spoke with another line sister who confirmed what I had been told. I had not ever lost anyone close to me and had no idea of how to handle it. I knew that there must have been some error, so I called Nadine's cell phone. There would never be another moment that I could speak to Nadine in this life, and my heart broke. When we attended her funeral, my heart broke even more. I refused to view her beautiful resting spirit, because I refused to acknowledge this as truth. All I had ever known to do was to reject pain, and this was far too much to bear. Nadie was vibrant, hopeful, spiritual, cultured, and understood more than any of the older girls how to live in the moment and embrace life.

I returned home to discover that I was pregnant. My husband and I were overjoyed, because we had made no plans for a new baby. We instantly attached to the possibilities of a new addition. This gave me great joy and helped me to see that life consisted of evolution. Although I could not make sense of the loss of Nadine and the hole in my heart, I learned to speak to her every day as I would the baby growing inside of me.

I guessed that this baby would be a son. For months, we nurtured the baby and began to make preparations. Our family was excited to say the least. As I went for my doctor's appointment in anticipation of the new developments, I remember beginning to think of names as I walked into the office. I left work to attend this appointment and told my husband that I would call him with all of the updates since he had such a long commute. This visit would allow me to see the baby through ultrasound, and I lived to see my babies moving around. It made the experience even more real. As I lay on the table in the midst of the ultrasound, the nurse changed her demeanor. She seemed to be in search. "Is everything okay?" I asked. No answer. I was so certain that things were okay that I comforted her. "I'm sure everything is fine. Should I lay differently?" I asked. The quiet that filled the room was horrid. The words that she spoke killed my spirit: "The baby doesn't have a heartbeat. I'm so sorry." I became paralyzed. The nurse instructed me to place my clothes back on and come inside the doctor's quarters. I did so, and the doctor began to explain what had happened to me. I heard silence. She provided me with some papers that would direct me to schedule a surgical procedure that would extract the pregnancy, because it was no longer valid.

I left the doctor's office again in a state of confusion. Life had again slipped out of my hands.

On our sixth anniversary, my husband and I sat in the hospital, because my body had made the decision to extract the pregnancy on its own. Mentally, I was not present. I cried for days on end. Giving up was never an option, because I had a husband and two children who were counting on me and I would never let them down, but the pain that I felt was unbearable.

Six months later, we found out that we were pregnant again. The pain from the loss of Nadine and the baby had impacted me so much that I never even acknowledged the pregnancy in public. My husband, mother, and I were the only ones who knew. My husband would always ask, "When are you going to tell people?" The pain wouldn't allow me to accept the baby, because I lived each day in fear that the same series of events might transpire. I loved the baby growing inside of me with all of my heart and read and sang and nurtured, but I could not allow myself to be vulnerable. I could not bear such pain again. The same wall that I had placed in many volatile relationships was the same wall that I had assembled in my soul. I continued working out, lifting weights, and doing squats daily. The only comfort that I knew was to keep life the same. Around the seventh month, my staff at my then job began to ask if I was pregnant. I never answered. I never acknowledged.

Around the eighth month of pregnancy, I had to be hospitalized for dehydration. While lying in the hospital bed receiving treatment, I made a promise to God, myself, and the baby growing inside of me: "God, let your will be done." I acknowledged that I did not have the power to change the will of God. I addressed the past hurt and said a prayer to release the spirit of the baby that had departed from pain. I also took action and began to make plans for the new baby that would arrive. We found out that she would be a girl. I began to restore the dreams that I had for my first daughter, Lauren, to have a sister.

On our seventh anniversary, God gave us London Blake Orie. One year later from the date that our baby had departed this life, he gave us life.

Today, I keep Nadine's picture in a treasure box that I look at every day. I speak to her candidly and laugh at the many ways that I know she would respond. Oddly enough, London embodies many of the same characteristics that made Nadine so special. Every day around her is a party. She sings and dances and lights up the room with every breath. I cannot imagine life without my children, and I could not have imagined life not having met Nadine. I know the beautiful baby that we lost sits in his Aunt Nadine's lap, and they laugh at us. They watch over us, and they protect us.

From the pain emerges passion to accept the will of the universe and to live every moment with vigor, for pain is the essence of passion and purpose.

A heroine in heels turns pain into prosperity.

A Heroine in Heels: Arthlene LeGair

Bound, broken, and wrapped in chains. That could be said of Arthlene's mindset when she found herself in the midst of a verbally abusive relationship. You're not beautiful, you're fat, and you're never going to succeed—these were the words that were so harshly spoken to and often owned by Arthlene. With the weight of responsibility that a family brings, staying was the only option.

There are times that even in the midst of the darkness of pain, a beam of light shines through so brilliantly that it cannot be ignored. Arthlene LeGair was not a woman who was bound, broken, and wrapped in chains; she was a heroine who did not recognize the magnitude of her power. After shopping for a dress for her then teen daughter to attend homecoming, she was appalled at the lack in modesty in formal wear for young ladies. With no formal seamstress training, Arthlene harnessed her inner heroine and began to design a dress that would resonate with a teen audience but also one that she could be proud to clothe her daughter in for such a momentous occasion. At first sight of the dress designed by Arthlene, people began to inquire where the dress was purchased. It was in that moment that she acknowledged her power and began her evolution into a self-taught seamstress and couture designer. From her source of pain, Arthlene created the LeGair Luxury Brand, a passion that would set the world of fashion on fire.

My first face-to-face meeting with Arthlene would further prove why she is a heroine in heels. I had previously requested to interview Arthlene to be featured in my documentary *I AM*, featuring the Consciously Beautiful Movement. When I arrived at her boutique, the LeGair Luxury Brand Boutique, I would later learn that a critical staff member would not be in attendance. Inside, I panicked, but outside, I attempted to appear calm. In truth, I felt a sense of defeat as I thought that my day of filming and potentially the entire project would come to a screeching halt.

For some reason, the spirit of discernment came over her, and she requested to grab the hands of everyone involved with the project to pray. In a magical moment, she revealed her most powerful weapon to all of us: prayer. Honey, Ms. Arthlene put down a prayer like nobody's business. She prayed that any forces that would come to harm the project would all be denounced and depowered.

After her prayer, the entire crew felt a unique sense of authority. She singlehandedly calmed the raging storm that no one had even warned was coming. I firmly believe that iron sharpens iron, and I would request her presence and prayer many more times. I seek her words and wisdom in times of happiness and despair. Arthlene LeGair is renowned for transferring power to empower (let that sink in).

From her source of pain, Arthlene gave birth to her greatest passion and purpose.

AHIH Tip: Surround yourself with people who transfer power to empower.

Arthlene LeGair

"Sometimes the struggle that we go through is to help empower someone else."

CHAPTER 3

Hope

Hope
hōp/
noun
"A feeling of expectation and desire for a certain thing to happen."⁵

Hope breathes life into our hearts.
—Ardre Orie

My heart breeds hope as we breathe air. Everything that I contemplate and feel within my heart stems from hope. For me, hope is the nucleus of my soul and envelopes all that I have ever aspired to be and do, including that of which I am unaware.

The impact that my actions have on the world are grounded in hope. Hope illuminates our path, for we walk in darkness.

In January 2015, I established the #IAM500 Campaign solely in the element of hope. The #IAM500 Campaign would offer 500 free makeovers and empowerment sessions to 500 women and teen girls. When I announced that I would embark upon this mission, the only certainty intact was my hope to accomplish such a great feat.

Annually, I host the Consciously Beautiful Heart 2 Heart Retreat. The retreat is an event that brings women and teen girls from all walks of life from all over the United States and a growing number of ladies who travel internationally together for a heartfelt weekend of inspirational highs and lows with one goal: for women and teen girls to reevaluate their value and love of self. During the weekend, we host a special event called The Consciously Beautiful Day of Glamour. One year in particular, I had just hosted my first play, Lipstick Monologues, as the opening event, and I was extremely tired the next morning. I arrived at the Consciously Beautiful Day of Glamour with no makeup as did all of the women. We arrive with no makeup as this is symbolic of a "blank canvas." During the event, we share, laugh, cry, and detox emotionally. As we transitioned to the segment in which all of the women receive makeovers, I was moved in observation of the looks on the beautiful faces of the ladies and teens who attended. It was priceless. About mid-way through the day, an amazingly beautiful lady, a single mother who had just been pampered, leaned over to me and, while looking in the mirror, said, "This was so amazing; I still can't believe that it is me." She went on to ask, "When are you getting your makeup done?" This moment was significant for two reasons: She was a single mother, highly educated, and worked extremely hard to ensure that her daughter had all that she needed and wanted and that she could provide an amazing life for them. Because of the fact that she was a professional woman who appeared to have it all together, she rarely received the gift of someone taking time to do something for her. So many strong women are recognized as those who don't need help. This couldn't be further from the truth, because no matter how strong we are, it always feels good when people take just a moment to make us feels special and worthy. This was also a pivotal moment for me, because, as I looked around the room, the women (many who had arrived with heads down or those who shed tears as they revealed their personal struggles and stories) were laughing, sharing, and exchanging with each other.

In that moment, nothing mattered except the fact that we all felt good about ourselves and worthy of extending words of support and encouragement to each other.

That moment gave me an infinite sense of hope, because I envisioned myself creating that moment for so many more women—hence the birth of the #IAM500 Campaign.

Watching them gave me hope in knowing that I was doing the work that I was placed here to do but also that there was more to be done, and, although I didn't know how, I felt a strong sense of hope that I would somehow figure it out. I now acknowledge hope as an expectation. We must expect the things that we hope for, or they will not come to fruition. We must then follow up our hope with work. As the good book says, "Faith without works is dead."

I now know that my work is a direct result of my faith. I now work with the expectation of harvest. Do you?

Struggling Artist

Sometimes I hope so hard that it hurts. When I see the traces of what could be, I am left with only my thoughts. I transfer every thought into action, but there is only so much that I can do without you. I have no ownership of the riches or resources of this world. You own it all.

Sometimes I hope so hard that it hurts. You have created and resurrected greatness in me, and, every second and minute of every day, I want to create. In this place, I have profound freedom that money can't buy. I know that to create is to be one with God.

My soul aligns with the universe, for I was created to create. Sometimes I hope so hard that it hurts. I want others to see exactly what I see and feel what I feel. I kneel before the heavens with a humble plea:

Can the world find value in what I create so that I too can eat? My gifts are invaluable, worth more than precious rubies or gold; please, oh please, Lord, let my work be sold. Help me to inherit the riches of the earth for discovering what I was placed here to do since my birth. Don't let me die with nothing on my plate. Open up the heavens and pour me out a blessing, for, no matter what happens, I will hope, I will wait, I must create.

A Heroine in Heels: Alima Albari

My first encounter as a newbie in the makeup and beauty industry was working with Alima. I was introduced to her by a college classmate and friend named Keri Stewart, whom I adore. Keri always understood my vision and would do anything within her reach to be a part of the provision. Needless to say, I trusted her judgment. I had just launched my cosmetics line I Love Me and needed to put together all of the visuals that would let the world know that we were open for business. Upon first meeting, I knew that Alima was extremely busy, and I would later learn that she ran Alima Industries, a multimedia talent agency and home to a plethora of established and rising stars.

Our first event together was a photo shoot and casting call, and it was a major success with an overwhelming turnout. From that moment on, I could see that Alima was excited about the future of my company and believed in my vision. It was equally apparent that she did not get excited about projects that were spearheaded by lackluster leaders. She, too, shared a keen sense of discernment. As time passed and we worked on several projects together, I came to realize that if she was going to work for the success of a project, she had to know with certainty that the one who gave birth to it would do the same. Her drive and determination was unmatched. You could see the hope in her eyes. Throughout the course of our professional relationship, we began to bond, and Alima disclosed to me that she was a survivor of domestic violence. It all made sense. She made the most of every moment, because she realized how quickly things could change. I asked Alima what she felt the most important lesson that she gleaned from the relationship that she had the power to escape from, and she replied: "I learned that self-love and forgiveness are the most important things. I've learned that we can all lose sight of hope because of the things that we experience, but it is the only thing that truly allows us to move forward."

Alima would take time to teach me the ropes, showing me what to look for in pictures and how to ensure a successful on-set experience. I was a quick study, and I knew for a fact that I was going to be successful in this industry, not because I was overly confident, but because I knew that I had found my lane. Alima and I would later find that we shared a sentiment that was absolutely priceless: confidence in our ability to make things happen. Fast forward several years and I've witnessed her create major productions in the music and film industry in moments of prosperity and times of famine. I've witnessed her turn small budgets into polished, finished products. I've witnessed her seamless execution of being a creative director on set to taking control of the camera at a photo shoot and mastering the photography. She can do it all. But of all the messages that she has subliminally spoken to me, her actions spoke loud and clear: "Never give up." If you can see beyond what is in front of you, if you have the ability to hope beyond your current disposition, your dream will never die. Alima embodies hope. Her vision and her work will live eternally.

Alima Albari

"Be exactly who you are and love it."

CHAPTER 4

Fear

Fear

ˈfir/

noun

"An unpleasant emotion caused by the belief that someone or something is dangerous, likely to cause pain, or a threat."[6]

Fear is a leisurely drive down the highway of insecurity.
—Ardre Orie

Diane von Furstenberg, acclaimed designer noted as the creator of the wrap dress that glides on and makes women feel feminine and invincible all at once, was quoted as saying: "I didn't always know what I wanted to do, but I knew the kind of woman I wanted to be."

The root of all evil in my opinion is fear. It is the black jelly bean, the taboo topic, the words left unspoken. Fear can create a plethora of emotions and sentiments, but the most powerful of them is insecurity.

When our actions are rooted in fear, we simply cannot win.

I could write an entire book about fear, but the most sentimental story that I can share is about a woman named JoAnn. Her dark hue was pure and unforgiving. A subtle shade of brown with undertones of love. JoAnn grew up in a time where her skin was not valued reverenced for its beauty. She was often led to believe that she was not beautiful from those who are most influential in a child's life: teachers and family members who demonstrated their lack of compassion and non-acceptance of the very essence of who she was. JoAnn was the only child of an educator who spent a great deal of time with her grandparents in the early years of her life. She would grow up with an absent father, and, at present, she recalls that she had only seen a picture of him once.

In spite of it all, she successfully pursued Bachelor's and Master's degrees in Guidance and Counseling. Throughout her career, she provided her powerful spirit of discernment and listening ear to several families, students, and friends for well over thirty-five years as a guidance counselor in the public school system. Even today, as she frequents local eateries and shopping centers in her community, the traces of her work are ever present as children and adults shout "hello" or run to give her a hug—all former students whose lives she positively impacted.

During her early years of college, JoAnn married and gave birth to her first child and only son. Upon realizing that the marriage would not work, she continued her education and amicably parted ways with her then husband. After the completion of her collegiate studies, JoAnn relocated from Georgia to Florida and met the father of her only daughter.

From birth to adulthood, JoAnn had acquired many insights from life about relationships and learned many hard lessons. She watched and often became the center of countless domestic disputes between her mother and stepfather. What she knew for certain was how to recognize dysfunction, which became her passion in counseling others through theirs.

In many instances, we possess the tools to save others but find those tools incompetent in saving ourselves.

JoAnn would give birth to her only daughter and vowed to break every chain and source of dysfunction that had been present in her life. This critical moment in her life would revolutionize her legacy.

Like many of us, a reigning theme in JoAnn's experience with relationships was fear. Fear to love wrong. Fear to love and lose. Fear of self-love. Like a tidal wave, JoAnn made a decision to turn fear into fuel and insecurity into intelligence and used them as the guiding principles from which to raise her daughter.

Day in and day out, leading by example, she instilled the virtue of hard work, merit, and pride within her daughter. JoAnn worked several jobs simultaneously to ensure that her daughter would never lack the experiences and vantage from which to attain success. Her daughter would accompany her at many of her evening employment experiences and saw with her own eyes work ethic at its epitome. Her daughter would learn the power of persistence.

JoAnn's toil would manifest in successfully assisting her daughter to complete high school and college. He daughter would go on to earn three degrees and infinite power to walk fearlessly through life.

JoAnn Jenkins is my mother, the essence of who I am and the rationale for this book. Mothers are often seen as heroines, but I am able to easily identify and recognize heroic qualities, because I have witnessed the epitome of heroic efforts. I have observed the journey, and, most importantly, I recognize that the heroic life is a marathon, not a sprint. For those who acknowledge their inner heroine, they also recognize that "easy" is not a path of choice nor an option. For those of us willing to take the leap of faith in absence of the parachute and those of us willing to build wings on the way down—we must push, fight, and persevere. The amazing feats that can be accomplished are unfathomable. JoAnn Jenkins turned fear into fuel and insecurity into intelligence and used them as the guiding principles to become the heroine of her own life and mine. Because of her heroic efforts, I will use every ounce of my energy to help other women and girls channel the innate power that lies within each of us.

Although I tell her often, I am also writing with an immense sense of pride that it may be immortalized:

JoAnn Jenkins dedicated her life to instilling infinite power within the generations of her lineage. I live fearlessly, because she taught me how.

A Heroine in Heels: Arnita Johnson

I would venture to say that many of our actions are the result of fear. From the moment we see something that we like or witness someone who has what we believe to be good or profound, our fear launches.

It's as though we fear not being enough, not having enough, not being worthy enough, not amounting to enough. Fear and insecurity are the root of all evil.

It has been my experience that there are gods and angels that walk the earth. Gods lead and impart vision within us. Angels save us from ourselves, protect us from our demons, and illuminate a path that we may follow.

Arnita Johnson is an angel in every sense of the word. Upon our first correspondence, I knew that she was authentic. I believe that a heroine in heels has no need to be anything other than herself, for she is confident in who and what she is. A heroine in heels is comfortable with her earthly assignment and purpose and assumes responsibility for the mission that she is to fulfill.

Initially, I was asked if I would like to interview Arnita for the Consciously Beautiful Movement by her publicist Lillie Mae of Lillie Mae PR. Lillie Mae provided me with a briefing explaining that Arnita was the founder of Luxurious Credit and that she helped customers and clients to improve their overall credit rating.

I found this to be intriguing, because we don't often associate luxury with good credit, but we should.

From the moment that we said "hello" on the phone, I knew that we would be friends. Her first words were these: "Hey, girl, I am so excited to participate in your movement; this is amazing!" It was as if we had known each other for years. She went on to express how much it meant to her to have an opportunity to think about beauty and self-worth. Her personality was kind, gentle, and, most importantly, authentic.

I can't stress enough how much it means to come face to face with authenticity in a day and age where social media allows us to be whoever we want to be, make up allows us to look however we want to look, and reality shows and media allow us to create false hope and innuendos in our own lives.

This was just the beginning of the layers of Arnita. We swapped life stories and vowed to always remain in touch.

A few weeks later, I would have the opportunity to meet Arnita in person. This time, I would witness her in action as a keynote speaker. During her presentation, she candidly expressed the difference between a life of prosperity and a life of poverty. Her innate power would be further revealed not by what she said but by what she did.

After speaking, she and I chatted and decided to schedule her interview for later date. She was exhausted as she had flown from Texas to Atlanta with very little sleep. My attention was drawn to the countless ladies that approached her with questions about solving their credit woes. Although her business Luxurious Credit was built on providing the same advice to paid clients, she willingly gave of herself for free. In the midst of her exhaustion, she continued to give as she answered questions to save women. It was as if she wore a cloak and others wanted to just touch the hem; she was an angel.

Arnita represents the dismissal of fear, the lighthouse at the end of the dark sea. For so long, people have been haunted by their past credit mistakes that led to their future demise. Arnita and her Luxurious Credit team spend their days down in the trenches lifting others out. Arnita understands the improvement in the quality of life for those who choose to live with good credit.

Arnita developed her business out of a personal need as she recognized that her life was stifled due to poor credit. While working at a local car dealership, she scrutinized the treatment of those with good credit versus those with poor credit, only to realize that good credit would alleviate a life of fear and insecurity due to finances.

Arnita now travels from state to state educating the masses through her Cupcakes and Credit seminars.

In addition to Luxurious Credit, Arnita recently acquired the company Belladonna Extensions, a luxury hair line providing extensions for women and hair care providers.

Arnita also launched a campaign to show people how to save their money. She ventured on a personal mission to save $1,000 monthly. With her saved money, she established Worth the Investment, a fund that donates $1,000 per month to female business owners who demonstrate their willingness to help others.

Arnita is showing the world how to take control of their lives by harnessing the power writhing to live a life free from financial fear. Arnita is an angel and a heroine in heels.

Arnita Johnson

I wake up in a dream everyday. Unimaginable opportunities fall into my lap. I often think about all of the times that I was going to give up. I just thank God that He never gave up on me.

CHAPTER 5

Envy

'envē/

noun

"A feeling of discontented or resentful longing aroused by someone else's possessions, qualities, or luck."[7]

I bear no fruit from other seeds, only that from which I was created.
—Ardre Orie

I remember how many times I felt different growing up and in school. I worked extremely hard to be like everyone else. Extremely hard. In my community, being different could and often did lead to scrutiny.

There was something about me that was a little different.

We often confuse different with better, but this is a moot point. Different in that I had aspirations that only I could dream of. Again, not because I was special but because they were visions given only to me.

I did not want to be a product of my environment.

The constant bullying and revelations that girls wanted to harm me were unreal. I had never dated anyone else's boyfriend and never willingly or knowingly done hurtful things to others.

I could never understand why I was ridiculed and isolated for being who I was.

I recall vividly being called into the principal's office to be told that I would no longer be able to attend my high school's basketball games, because it was a safety hazard. There were too many other young ladies that had it in for me.

To put things into perspective, I was Student Body President. I had won votes from the majority of the students to serve in a leadership capacity, but there was a minority that did not agree with who I was or wanted to be.

I had dreams beyond my city. For this very reason, like many young people, I tortured myself mentally to figure out how to just fit in.

The last thing that I needed in the midst of adolescence was to stand out more.

I would later learn that this thing that made me different was my "light." We all have one. However, we sometimes allow others to dim it, or we dim it ourselves.

Furthermore, I would later learn that I was a victim of envy.

Like poison ivy, envy is dangerous when rubbed against our spirits.

When we become envious of others, it drives us to think, speak, and behave in ways that are not representative of who we truly are.

I did not have anything better than any of the young ladies who caused me so much grief. I can honestly say that those tumultuous years left me with such a bittersweet taste in my mouth for my hometown.

I would leave gladly for college at Florida State University and walk into a new world filled with possibilities.

In this environment, most recognized these lights, and everyone walked around with their light glowing like a halo. Everyone in this environment had goals and aspirations beyond their current disposition. Everyone wanted more from life and recognized that life had more to offer if you were willing to work for it.

In this environment, the word "envy" would appear to be a thing of the past. It disappeared into the deep forest of drive and determination that fueled my future and I was non longer a victim of my past..

True Colors

I want what she has, but I am too proud to admit it.

I've got green on my hands.

I wanted to congratulate her, but she had enough people to tell her how amazing she was already.

I've got green on my hands.

I'm kind of sick of seeing her. The vision of her face is becoming a constant reminder of just how much I am being overlooked.

I've got green on my hands.

I just don't understand what everyone sees in her that they don't see in me.

I've got green on my hands.

I'm not going to support her; I've got my own dream to build.

I've got green on my hands.

Oh, you thought what she did was amazing? I call it average at best.

I've got green on my hands.

I deserve to be honored and recognized for my work, but we keep seeing her. I wholeheartedly disagree.

I've got green on my hands.

I have come to the conclusion that you don't have to like everybody, and that's okay. She was never a true friend to me anyway.

I've got green on my hands.

I just want my time to shine, my name written in lights. I just want the same thing that she is getting out of life. She looks so happy, and I, too, deserve this joy. I've worked so hard in silence, but, today, I want more. Today, I want to have my moment for life, but this green on my hands won't stop causing me grief and strife.

You see, the more I think of her, the less I think of me, and every bit of my joy is being stolen by the thief.

This green on my hands is only a disguise for the envy that I so often deny. I am envious of her, because I have not recognized my own value; for if I did, there would be no need to compare. What is for her is for her and me for me, no true need to stop and stare.

Envy is a dangerous color, and it holds us back on our journey. What is for her is for her and me for me, no true need to compare. Comparison is the thief of joy, and that's the end of the story.

I wash my hands again, and my life changes in an instant: I congratulate, celebrate, and honor her, because she deserves it. My light begins to shine so bright that it illuminates the room. I am who I am and have learned to take pride in watching my flowers bloom.

My hands are no longer green with envy; today, they are as white and pure as snow. A blank canvas available for life to write and me to show. I am open to my journey and I lift my hands to the sky. What is for me is for me, and I now know that I won't be denied.

My hands are no longer green with envy, they are as white and pure as the snow. What is for me is for me and I release all traces of envy, she doesn't live here anymore..

A Heroine in Heels: Koereyelle DuBose

A woman who is passionate about her purpose is what I call a queen. I was introduced to Koereyelle by a mutual sorority sister named A Lekay, founder of Illusions by A. Lekay Swimwear. It is imperative that I mention this, because, as I always say, iron sharpens iron. A heroine in heels recognizes the power of connections and is a connector.

Koereyelle would also prove to be a connector in my life.

Our first meeting was at a little cafe in Atlantic Station in Atlanta, Georgia. That cafe would become where we would exchange ideas, inspire each other, and vent. It is beyond necessary that like-minded energy is exchanged and is safe to do so.

Through our exchanges, Koereyelle made it clear that she was single but wanted to be married. Her experiences had taught her to be specific about what she was looking for in life and in a relationship. Koereyelle had learned to look beyond the dreaded "list" that so many single women conjure up. In her words: "I had a list and found who I thought was the one. He matched the list perfectly. However, I forgot to consider all of the things that were a part of his character that the list didn't include. Those are the things that we often forget to consider."

Koereyelle wanted not only to be married but also to become the best version of herself prior to doing so. Her mission allowed her to channel her intentions into power. With this power, she founded The Single Wives Club. The Single Wives Club was established with the following goals:

- To equip women with the skills necessary to be successful wives.
- To decrease the national divorce rate by increasing the number of loving, lasting relationships.
- To increase the number of happy, healthy children by creating happy, healthy homes.

Koereyelle grew The Single Wives Club from a potluck dinner with girlfriends into a corporation with international membership and a myriad of program offerings for the empowerment of women.

As opposed to being bitter or envious of relationships around her when her engagement ended, Koereyelle found insurmountable strength within to make a positive difference in her own life as well as the lives of others. Herein lies our greatest source of power: creating purpose from impactful living that helps others.

How did Koereyelle define "envy"? What had she learned early in life to equip her for moments like these?

When asked what "envy" meant, Koereyelle had the following to say: "'Envy' means ungrateful. You're so busy focusing on what someone else has that you forget to appreciate all that you have."

In an act of appreciation and recognition, I learned that Koereyelle wittingly leveraged partnerships and collaborations of value. She took note of the work ethic of others and aligned herself only with those who shared similar goals. Envy was not welcomed in Koereyelle's camp, only love and empowerment.

Today, you can find Koereyelle diversifying her portfolio and capitalizing on opportunities to turn her passion into profits. To date, she has launched three ventures:

- The Single Wives Club

The Single Wives Club educates, empowers, and inspires single ladies to become better women before becoming wives by living happy, healthy, wealthy lives.

- Ready to WERK

Ready to WERK was established to educate entrepreneurs on efficient and effective ways to build their brand on a reasonable budget.

- The Success Circle Network

The mission of The Success Circle Network is to connect like-minded women for powerful partnerships. Created by Koereyelle DuBose and Arnita Johnson, the movement provides a platform for women to share success secrets, support one another, and collaborate instead of compete.

Through many of our intimate conversations, we would share strategies for overcoming some of the most difficult moments that are common to those who dare to pursue their dreams, and one resounding theme is always present: "Drive in your lane." When your focus remains on driving in your own lane, there is very little room to be concerned with what is going in the cars surrounding you. You must wear blinders until you reach your destination. Koereyelle offers the following advice to alleviate envy:

"Think about your secret sauce; what makes you unique? There's something about you that no one can do better. Find that and focus on it whenever you feel insecure."

When asked what she would like her legacy to be, Koereyelle responded: "I would like to be remembered for changing society's perception of single women. You're not crazy if you're single past twenty-five; you have no reason to feel less than, and it's okay to be patient enough not to settle. My legacy will be one of empowerment and education."

To Koereyelle's point, I would be remiss if I did not acknowledge the opportunities that she extended to me to connect with like-minded individuals and exchange energy to increase my territory. I knew without question that Koereyelle could grasp the magnitude of my vision but more importantly that she would willingly act upon synergistic power to achieve our common goals. I will long remember her kindness.

A heroine in heels recognizes that we were never placed here to focus on our own agendas. We are here to unwrap the gift of a purpose greater than ourselves. Koereyelle understands that there is work to be done and that comparison, envy, and stagnation are all family members that she refuses to adopt. In the meantime, you can find her creative genius at work on a relentless mission to empower women and create opportunities to generate wealth.

In her words, I say, "WERK."

Koereyelle DuBose

Comparison will kill your spirit. You miss out on enjoying your life when you are so focused on others.

CHAPTER 6:

Pride

Pride

prīd/
noun
"A feeling or deep pleasure or satisfaction derived from one's own achievements, the achievements of those with whom one is closely associated, or from qualities or possessions that are widely admired."[8]

> *Pride is the counterpart to confidence.*
> —Ardre Orie

To the contrary, the world continues to teach us to be boastful. The consummate use of social media rewards us for sharing our accomplishments, thoughts, feelings, and even our most intimate moments in life.

Pride, however, is silent. It is the detail that is derived from success and the relative of confidence. The observation of pride can easily be missed but not mistaken. Pride is the essence of those who have work by those who pay close attention to life's most important details. It is the words unspoken.

Aside from having a marriage that has withstood the test of time and three amazing children, one of my proudest moments was the completion of my first book, *Consciously Beautiful: I Am Enough*.

I remember when I received my first copy at my doorstep. I opened the box, and, like a child's first visit to a candy store, I absolutely could not believe my eyes. The most roaring revelation that this accomplishment would document was that I had discovered what I was good at. More importantly, I would accept my destiny as a writer. Even my then editor told me that he believed that writing was my lane. This book represented what I had known for many years but had not pursued with all my might. To this day, my husband encourages me to write, and, as an avid reader, he suggests new techniques and genres for me to pursue.

The revealing truth of the matter is that after leaving my job, I pursued money. My goal was to make money. I am certain that most entrepreneurs would disagree with me, but the sense of pride that I felt in writing the book demonstrated that I was most proud when my purpose was rooted in something more meaningful. Pride for me would have to be irrefutably rooted in my willingness to make a difference. Opening the box and holding the book in my hands was a moment of clarity.

I had often confused pride with my ability to generate an income. In the past, I had been proud of myself when I increased my salary. I had been most proud of myself in the moments that I could see the financial impact that my toil had for my family. I had been most proud of being able to make purchases and revel over material things. Back then, my pride was immature. When my family and I made the decision to put family first and I resigned from my position, I had a larger-than-life plan to make those around me proud by generating my same salary (that I had worked for well over eight years to build) in one year through entrepreneurship with a husband, three children (one of whom was a newborn), and a move to a new city with no friends or relatives. That sounds possible, right? When I failed miserably to generate the amount of money truly needed to run my business and irrefutably struggled to do so, I felt that same feeling of worthlessness that I had felt so many times in the past. My sense of pride had been completely depleted, and I wanted to give up. That same year, I had spoken to, touched, and impacted well over 500 girls, traveling from city to city speaking and hosting seminars.

My family sacrificed as I would often leave my husband and two children behind, fly with the newborn baby to each city to be of service. In my daughter London's first two years of life, she flew approximately twenty-four times.

After the first year, I did not meet my financial goals, but I did not give up, because I felt like I was so close. After the second year, I did not meet my financial goals, and I did not give up, but, admittedly, I was not proud of myself or what I had accomplished. In hindsight, I felt like a complete failure.

What I did not take time to notice was the impact that I had made on the lives of the young ladies who I set out to inspire and empower. I had always been sincere about wanting to make a difference in the lives of others, but my measure of success that would allow me to experience a sense of pride was rooted in money.

Holding the book in my hands was a clear message from God that my pride must be rooted in things that are not tangible. I now recognize that I was not placed on earth to generate money but to serve others. My sense of pride is now grounded in making an impact and being of service. I am still a work in progress, but, each day, I set out with a mission to serve. In this space, I have generated more income that I was ever in danger of generating when money was my focus.

The Mountain Top

When I get to the mountain top, there will be no need to scream. I've walked a thousand miles with the weight of these hopes, aspirations and dreams.

Along my way the weight got so heavy that I wanted to turn around but I always remembered to look up and the sun remembered to shine down.

I built my strength climbing this mountain. I took every step with pride. The grit and gumption showed me exactly who I was inside.

There was never any competition, I walked this mountain alone. Every person has a climb that is all their own. So when I get to the mountain top, there will be no need to scream for I will stand in God's glory and fulfill every hope, aspiration and dream.

A Heroine in Heels: Raven Clements Thomas

Sturdy yet gentle.

The most profound kind of beauty is effortless.

I met Raven in college as we pledged the same sorority. Anyone that knows her intimately would agree that the woman she is today, is exactly who she has always been.

Have you ever noticed that those who are truly comfortable in their own skin make the least noise?

Raven, a football-loving, trash-talking woman of divine spirituality, statuesque and divine, spoke her mind but never spoke in vain. While many women spend time amidst cat fights, it was always clear that she was in competition with no one. She knew her worth, and it was never up for debate. These same skills would transcend her life as a wife, mother, and bona fide entrepreneur.

I kept in touch with Raven through social media, and we always connected as I believe that light attracts light. We both recognized the struggles that accompany putting your family over your career and the undeniable balancing act that accompanies the pursuit of a dream. We would converse back in forth and engage in group discussions. To take it a step further, we shared an infinite love for our alma mater, Florida State University. Quietly, Raven would build a million-dollar business and open the hearts of entrepreneurial hopefuls right before our eyes.

She made a very humble post about her appearance on *Shark Tank*, and I along with all of our sorority sisters and America tuned in. She captivated the judges and gave an authentic pitch. No surprises, there. That day would exemplify the magnitude of Raven's quiet confidence which I now refer to as "pride." Mark Cuban, admired by every current, aspiring, and wanna-be entrepreneur, bit. If you don't know who Mark Cuban is, allow me to give you the Wikipedia definition:

> Mark Cuban is an American businessman, investor, and owner of the NBA's Dallas Mavericks, Landmark Theatres, and Magnolia Pictures, and the chairman of the HDTV cable network AXS TV. He is also a "shark" investor on the television series Shark Tank.

The bottom line is that, as I write this book, Mark Cuban is worth $2.7 billion dollars and shows no signs of slowing down. Mark Cuban saw Raven's pride.

In the business world, we always say that people don't do business with products; they do business with people. Mark Cuban wanted to do business with Raven. That night on *Shark Tank*, he would offer her exactly what she asked for: $100k for a 25 percent stake in her company The Painted Pretzel and her website shut down from all of the orders.

Prior to going on the show, The Painted Pretzel was already on the rise. Raven had managed to open her own storefront in Arizona and maintain product placements in stores like Neiman Marcus, Sac's Fifth Avenue, and many other fine stores in malls across America. Raven was also a top pick on *The Rachael Ray Show*.

The problem with Raven's success is that it was growing faster than what she had the capacity to facilitate. Raven almost had to walk away from a two million dollar order from Sam's Club, a company owned by Wal-Mart.

The truth is you would never know that Raven was by reading any of her social media posts or in the midst of general interaction with her. I am reminded of a quote that I often say: "Confidence is silent." When you are on a divine track, the journey speaks for itself. This silent confidence translates to pride.

Raven was born into a large family, composed of four sisters and two brothers. Subconsciously, she watched her mother exemplify strength, courage, and endurance on a continual basis.

Most importantly, Raven recalls that her mother did not set barriers on her life and what she could accomplish.

Raven notes that from as early as she could remember she thrived on the notion that if you wanted something you should pursue it relentlessly. Through our conversations, I inquired about Raven's confidence and her thought process, to which she replied, "I've always believed that girls could do anything that boys could do." Another key notion that leads to the demonstration of Raven's heroism is her belief that failure is never permanent. Raven sees her plans as roadmaps and the occurrence of a detour has no bearing on her ability to arrive at her final destination. This process of thinking could curtail much of the disdain that many feel prior to giving up.

There is a profound level of peace that Raven innately possesses. It is almost indescribable. Raven acts with certainty of success and captures life's moments with confidence all while intentionally navigating a path that is divinely ordered. I simply refer to this notion of living life and demanding only the best from it as pride. In this space, you know your worth, your work, and your final destination.

Raven is the epitome of pride. She moves in silence and let's her unquestionable success speak for itself.

Raven Clements Thomas

I've been asked whom my competitors are and I can honestly say that I do not know. I've never been in competition with anyone. I've remained focused on achieving the goals that I've set for myself.

CHAPTER 7

Courage

Courage

cour·age
ˈkərij/
noun
"The ability to do something that frightens one."[9]

For women, courage is not optional.

It is as important as the oxygen we breathe.

—Ardre Orie

Coveted actress Ruby Dee was quoted as saying, "God, make me so uncomfortable that I will do the very thing that I fear."

I was well planned when it came to my professional journey. I went to Florida State University and earned a B.S. in Special Education. While there, I made the decision to further my education and earned my M.S. in Special Education. Upon graduation from college, I became a teacher. I married my high school sweetheart and couldn't see beyond our life that we began to create in that city. It was the first city that I lived in outside of my hometown, and, in my mind, I thought that it would be my last.

I began to grow my career and family and became content.

The news that my husband received a job in Tampa, Florida, was not only shocking but also left me feeling helpless and afraid. I did not have the courage to start over, interview for a new position, or pick up the pieces of the puzzle that I thought were so well put together.

In retrospect, this was senseless, because the relocation was an opportunity for our family to have a better quality of life. Like so many, I was blinded by my comfort zone.

Reluctantly, we moved, and I attended a job fair. I got a job and settled in to the fact that we could create a life in a new place. I was displeased with my job and felt a strong urge to affect more students than just those in my classroom, so I began pursuit of my Ed.S. in Educational Leadership. With a new baby and my husband working nights, I wasn't so sure if the move had been a mistake. It was uncomfortable. I never saw my husband, because he would have to sleep during the day when I worked, and then he would be leaving for work just as my daughter and I came home. I was afraid.

Upon completing my Ed.S., a light bulb went off that I could go beyond my classroom and become an administrator. This moment was significant, because fear becomes conquerable when we realize that we have the power to do so.

I was hired by an amazing angel named Krystal Carson to begin training to become an administrator. It was almost as if we were in a scene from *Rocky*. She taught me everything from how to walk in the room to the appropriate way to answer questions. She gave me countless opportunities to lead within our school. This was on-the-job training at its best.

As fate would have it, she experienced a severe tragedy that would require her to be away from the school, and I will never forget the words that she spoke to me: "I know you have everything under control, Mrs. Orie." From that moment, I exemplified a courageous educator and a candle was lit inside my soul. Two significant factors surfaced in the midst of this moment: I was prepared. I had put in the work to run the school in Ms. Carson's absence. This was not textbook knowledge; this was knowledge acquired from toil. I believe that A heroine in heels understands the value associated with experience acquired from toil. We don't just wake up ready for our greatest accomplishment; rather, we prepare for it.

The time soon came for me to interview for an actual position at another school. The lady who was once afraid of change was ready to meet the challenge. I was so prepared that during the screening, I made the highest score in the district. My success was not a result of me being special but more so a byproduct of the preparation and toil.

I worked for four years as an Assistant Principal and felt that there was nothing that I could not do in my role. From overseeing the safety of the entire school during lockdowns to assisting irate parents and students, I had the courage to do so. I walked into work each day with a cape on, at least that was the way that I felt. And then one day, everything changed.

During the summer of 2009, I was pregnant with my youngest daughter, London, and was in attendance at a training for administrators when I suddenly went into a state of seizure. I fainted and had to be transported via ambulance to the hospital. When I became coherent, I recall being on the stretcher and the Assistant Superintendent was standing over me instructing the ambulatory care team to take me to the hospital. I refused and sat up from the stretcher to say, "I don't need to go to the hospital. I need to stay and finish my training; today is the last day that it is being offered." Much to the surprise of the Assistant Superintendent and other bystanders, I had refused care for myself and my unborn child, because, in that moment, finishing my job was more important. Writing this truth makes me cringe. The dark truth is that, like many, I had become a slave to my job and could only see my worth in my ability to advance and achieve in my capacity as Assistant Principal.

In my grand scheme of plans, I believed that I would not miss a step when the baby was born and that I would work with even more vigor once she was born.

As I took the miserable drive in the ambulance to the hospital, I was alone as my husband had been notified and was en route. In this moment of silence, I remember a single tear streamed down my face. I realized that I lacked the courage to do anything other than what I had been doing in my present role, because it was all that I knew. I realized that I lacked the courage to fail. I lacked the courage to take the most precious time to grow, raise, and rear a family, because I did not want to "lose my space" at my job. All of the things that I was most afraid of surfaced along that dreaded ride.

As I lay in the hospital bed, my husband arrived. The sight of his face coupled with the movement of my unborn baby that let me know she was well would change the trajectory of my thought process and vibrations in my heart. From that moment on, I was courageous beyond measure, because I felt so strongly about my family and what I needed to be, give, and do to ensure that they were cared for, that my outlook on the capacity in which I would work would change forever. From that moment on, I knew in my soul it was possible that I would never return to my once coveted job. My courage led me to choose my family over my ambition which had once been the absolute driving force of my life.

Cross Country

Hey, baby! I've come a mighty long ways. I hit the open road traveling across country in search of my strength.

I've walked along a path lined with Afraid, frightened, and scared, but, at the rate I travel, they didn't stand a chance. Hey, baby! I've come a mighty long ways.

I've driven in a lane on the highway with Anxious, panicky, and petrified, but I veered off course. Those words are the exact opposite of what I've long been searching for. Hey, baby! I've come a mighty long ways.

I've since enhanced my vocabulary and expanded my horizons.

You can find me in the fast lane riding between Bold and brave.

I've even walked on the wild side with adventure, because now it's my middle name.

Hey, baby! I've come a mighty long ways.

Picture me rolling next to bravery, dauntless, and determination.

You see, my car's endurance bears the fortitude of grit.
I've got guts to last for days.

Hey, baby! I've come a mighty long ways.

I'm a lion-hearted hero with my heels on the gas.

Forget the open road, I'm traveling by sea, and, boy, am I moving fast.

Hey, baby! I've come a mighty long ways.

I'm on yacht with Spunk, stoutheartedness, and valor, and our hair is blowing in the wind.

Hey, baby! I've come a mighty long ways.

Far too often, I've been told that I'm taking too many trips.

But if you'd prefer we keep things simple, just know that I am on a lifelong road trip with my bestie who bears the name: Courage.

Hey, baby! I've come a mighty long ways.

A Heroine in Heels: Dar'shun Kendrick

I have always admired ladies who unapologetically speak their minds. I knew immediately that Dar'shun and I would be friends; she spoke her truths regularly. Our energy connected through social media, and I would invite her for lunch to learn more about her career path and understand her strength as one of the youngest African-American ladies to be elected to the Georgia House of Representatives, a move that I can only describe as courageous.

Dar'shun and I would go on to find many areas in which we could relate and develop a friendship filled with admiration. Our love for food and new dining experiences would be a source of connection forever.

As I grew to know Dar'shun, I observed that her courage appeared to be effortless. When asked what courage meant to her, she replied, "Keeping your promises no matter who disagrees with you." This explains the magnitude in which she serves as a state representative. Dar'shun found her power in being of service to the people whom she represented. She believed in her ability to make a difference.

She credits her parents for teaching her courage: "I was bullied as a child. Yet my mom told me to hold my head high and I did. I thank her for that because I am a much better person," said Kendrick.

Even in the midst of her daily activity, Dar'shun is forced to exude courage. She told me that she gets nervous when speaking in public, and I found it astonishing that she would select career paths that require so much of the very thing that frightens her. Dar'shun's educational qualifications speak for themselves:

- Master in Business Administration (Kennesaw State University)
- J.D. (University of Georgia)
- Bachelors of Arts (Oglethorpe University)

As an attorney, she inevitably speaks in court, and, as a state representative, she speaks when presenting bills.

I asked Dar'shun candidly why she would elect professions that require her to acknowledge her fears, to which she replied: "I am empowered to communicate what I believe and my political stance no matter who disagrees with me. I am unafraid to stand behind my beliefs and my word."

It is my belief that you can't have a conversation about courage without speaking about insecurities. Dar'shun noted that her biggest physical insecurity was that her ears poked out. When asked how she overcame her insecurity, she replied, "I just got over it. I'm smart." Conversations with Dar'shun were simple black and white. Could it be that we overcomplicate things so often that we paralyze ourselves and our potential?

Motivated by service to others, Dar'shun believes that fear is the factor that keeps us from becoming the absolute best versions of ourselves.

Furthermore, she notes that our insecurities make us less courageous and that they deserve less of a presence and voice in our lives.

Dar'shun believes that the world tells women that having too much courage is not desirable and is viewed as overly aggressive.

In true Dar'shun fashion, she states, "We lose our power by giving it to men."

The question that Dar'shun poses to women and girls everywhere is this: "Do you want fear to keep you from living the best life possible?"

"I want to have inspired people to overcome their circumstances and to become more than anyone could have imagined," states Kendrick.

I don't believe that Dar'shun has become more than what she imagined. It is because of her relentless display of courageousness that she has become exactly who she saw herself to be. If we adopt a spirit of fearlessness, the world is at our disposal. Imagine what you could do if you simply were not afraid.

Dar'shun Kendrick

To walk around in fear is a complete waste of our time and energy. Courage is our only option.

CHAPTER 8

Anger

an·ger
'aNGgər/
noun
"A strong feeling of annoyance, displeasure, or hostility."[10]

> *Anger is an overcast to life's possibilities. In the midst of it, the sun has no room to shine.*
>
> —Ardre Orie

I sat alone in my bedroom listening to threats of death and victimization. I knew that if I didn't do anything that he would kill her.

The rage that I felt in knowing that I would be forced to sacrifice my life and freedom for his senseless acts drove me to anger.

It is my belief that anger manifests in one of two ways, externally or internally.

I began to fail in school, disregard the wise council of adults, and exclude the thoughts of future plans. I would have to kill him, or he would kill my mother.

You never really know what hides behind a person's face. You never really know what hell breeds inside someone's home. Day in and day out, my mother and I would attend school and work as if nothing was happening. We appeared as normal as any other middle class family.

We spent the weekends in prison. We would be forced to walk to the nearest convenience store for food items as he would always take our only car, one which my mother had purchase with her blood, sweat, and tears, and leave us without transportation.

To add insult to injury, he would often pass by us on the street with other women in the car and not stop nor offer us a ride.

The sense of rage that I felt was insurmountable.

As the arguments and his bullying worsened, the anger turned to rage. I was motivated to plot a way to remove him. He had to expire for what he was doing to her. I was always raised to value human life. I believed it too precious and by no means were we as humans given the right to take control of another.

I openly admit that the anger would drive me to do anything to save her. She had dedicated all she had to me. She deserved to live. She did not deserve to be tortured anymore at the hands of a man who had no regard for her love.

My past experiences and my current situation had turned me against men. I hated them.

My point of no return was when I waited at school one day for her to pick me up. I waited for two hours, and she never came.

I was staying late at school, because I was forced to do additional work for extra credit. My teacher and I remained watchful for my mother to pick me up, but she never arrived.

Finally, my teacher offered to take me home, and I accepted. We drove to my home, which was a short distance from the school, and there was no car parked outside. I assumed she was not at home.

I used my key to unlock the door and instinctively called out, "Ma." There was no answer. As I walked down the hall, I was met only with silence and called her name again: "Ma." The silence remained.

As I glanced over, I saw a familiar body and began to speak. "Mom, why didn't you pick me up from school?" I was, in fact, angry because I felt like she left me hanging.

She never responded and never turned to look at me. I knew instantly that something was not right. Never in a million years could I prepare for what I would soon witness.

"Mom, I needed you to pick me up from school; where were you?" In that moment, my mother revealed her face from the shadow, and my heart sank into my feet. My soul was shattered and my hope diminished. Her eye was swollen so largely that she was unrecognizable. Her lip was split open and her heart broken. I saw the pain on her face. It was piercing.

All these nights I had prepared for this moment. I knew that this day would come, but no amount of preparation would have ever helped me in this moment.

I stood in silence. It was as if my heart stopped beating. This was death to me. The strongest most powerful person that I had ever known, my only hope, and the only person that I could lean and depend on was broken and so was I.

As it began to sink in, I remember that she had spent her life transferring power to me. She had taught me how to survive, how to maneuver in times of uncertainty. Most importantly, she taught me through her actions to never throw in the towel. A true heroine in heels never gives up.

Instantly, I helped her up from the corner; she didn't belong there. She was my queen, and she belonged on her throne. It was time for us to take back what rightfully belonged to us, our dignity.

From that moment on, we regained our power because we decided that we were powerful. We knew that for our circumstances to change, we must take responsibility and action to change them.

Unfortunately, my anger with him left me raped and robbed of my ability to recognize love. My anger hardened my heart.

I wrote a character named Ashli in my play *Lipstick Monologues* that describes what life would have been like had I acted in anger. Today, I live to tell the story. Today, my mother stands tall, strong, and proud: a survivor of domestic violence and self-esteem. Today, we both know our worth and that it can never be compromised. Today, she nor I give discounts, because our worth is invaluable.

A Heroine in Heels: Jill Tracey

Riding the momentum of the release of my first book, *Consciously Beautiful: I Am Enough*, I was invited to speak as a guest panelist for a youth summit in Miami by Alechia Reese, a positive woman with positive intentions who had founded a beautiful organization called The Girl Rethought Project. At the event, Jill came over to me and said, "Sista, I love that hair." My first interaction with her was the receipt and exchange of positive energy.

As the event ensued, I would later learn that Jill was an industry maven and was the acclaimed host of Hot 105 FM. At the close of the event, Alechia discreetly spoke to me saying, "Maybe you should give her a copy of your book."

Fast forward one year later, I randomly sent Jill a message about an idea that I had for collaboration. To my surprise, she was willing to take my call. When we engaged in our first conversation, there was instant synergy. I told Jill my dreams, and she listened. Shortly after I pitched my idea, she said, "What we can do is . . ."—and I immediately knew that she was on board. This was the start of something beautiful. Jill and I would schedule to talk every other week, and, although we were working on a project, we grew fond of the exchange. She would become what I now refer to as my "Fairy Godmother." She would teach and mentor me. The greatest gift that she has given me is reality. She does not sugarcoat the truth. She does not perch in the "amen choir." Instead, she is a realist that holds no bars. These are among the attributes that catapulted her career as a media maven. With over twenty years in the business, Jill Tracey is among the industry's most coveted personalities. Her presence at the industry's most exclusive events is highly sought after.

During one of our conversations, she expressed her disdain for the way the media industry can often treat women. She told me a story of a then director who attempted to belittle her in his truth. My heart hurt for her and all women as we are far too often subjected to the thoughts and sentiments of men whose opinions were never requested. In anger, I wrote a monologue that I pray one day I get to witness Jill perform.

It is raw, uncut, and real. Like Jill, this is not sugar coated but a beautiful revelation of what truly is.

Note: As a preface to the monologue, I must share the true backdrop. Jill was working and in conversation with her director when he looked at her and said, "You will never make it in this industry, because no one wants to *love* you." I have used the word "love" in place of the real word that he said as I know that all of my adult readers will be inclined to infer the true derogatory word used. However, I need for young ladies of all ages to be able to read and digest Jill's amazing display of heroism in hopes that she too might discover a part of herself.

Candy Coated

You'll never get far in this industry, because no one wants to *love* you.

Those were the last words that I heard before I blacked out.

Why would someone with so much power place such a heavy limitation on my life?

No one wants to *love* you.

It was almost as if I was destined for failure, a victim of circumstance and nature and a slave to the all-too-common perception that drives our values of what beauty is and should be.

I wondered if he knew then that I wasn't submitting my application for a beauty pageant. I was trying to follow my dreams of a career in media, but all I heard was "No one wants to *love* you."

That voice would haunt me night after night and fill my days with emptiness and despair. No one wants to *love* you.

I know I'm not alone as countless women are rejected because no one took the time to look beyond their full lips, hips, and the color of their skin. Far too many women are victimized and brutally attacked with vicious words that once spoken can never be taken back.

No one wants to *love* you—is that all you think of me?

But I do realize that that was then and this is now. Life has a funny way of circling us around.

Three hours and sixty seconds or 360 degrees, I must make you see that the precious gift of time has been so good to me. Time has been the best teacher, and this I have learned to be true: it was never really about loving me, because the story unfolded and didn't show much love to you.

I learned to bow my head, pray, and let my light so shine. I learned not to accept the hurt that others use to define.

No matter what has happened in my life or what hurtful event that could unfold, my reality is that I have always been the master of my fate. I have always been the captain of my soul.

Today, I sit perched on top of the world with music in my heart. I have but one wish for the women of the earth: Let no man or woman kill your spirit with words that are hurtful to your soul. Let no one place value when they have no knowledge of who you are or where you've been.

Every ounce of power that you need, you already have within.

No one wants to *love* you—those were the words that he said. Now, not one word penetrates the surface because I climaxed off of my success instead.

Through our exchanges, it was as if I was sitting at the feet of greatness; I was. Jill would share with me that growing up as an only child afforded her a life of confidence and access to many new things that others did not always have. In the same spirit in which she exists today, she always shared and enjoyed being a friend to many. Positive exchanges fill our cups indeed. As Jill matured, like many of us, the harsh realities of societally imposed beauties would make an unpleasant entrance and engulf her to become a victim. Like so many women, Jill said earnestly, "I never knew that there was anything wrong with my size until someone told me that there was." Jill went on to explain that her weight had always been a topic of concern for others. The harsh words of her former director would not be the only instance of scrutiny. Throughout her career, Jill was subjected to countless acts of detestable behavior from some of the industry's coveted personalities.

In spite of it all, Jill pushed through barriers relentlessly, opening doors for other women with color and curves. Even if it goes unspoken, Jill's presence, persistence, and endurance has paved the way for many.

Today, Jill travels in her own lane free from comparisons about her body or ability. Her presence commands love and acceptance. With a recently launched show *Behind the Mic*, she and I have decided to write her first book as well as an edition of *Lipstick Monologues*. There is so much more that the world must know about Jill Tracey.

A heroine in heels channels her anger into productivity. She does not allow it to consume her. Anger is fuel. Anger is drive. Anger is determination. Jill is now at the top of her game and climbing every day. A queen indeed.

Jill Tracey

We must be conscious, we must be aware of who we are and the value that we bring to our lives and the lives of others.

CHAPTER 9

Fatigue
Fa
/f
noun
"Extreme tiredness, typically resulting from mental or physical exertion or illness."[11]

No excuses, only plans.
—Ardre Orie

Multiple failures led me towards fatigue that would initiate thoughts of quitting. After working tirelessly to build the Pink Wish Foundation, the ends never seemed to meet. I established the Pink Wish Foundation in 2009 based upon a need to educate girls ages eight to eighteen about leadership and entrepreneurship and to decrease the occurrences of self-destructive behaviors often associated with the adolescent years.

I did everything that I thought needed to be done to grow a successful business venture. I attended every course on entrepreneurship that I could register for and commit to attending, applied for every grant and fellowship opportunity within my reach, and networked like a maniac. I still had not been able to raise the funding that I needed to pay staff and scale the business according to the business plan that I had invested so much into completing.

I saw others around me prosper, while I was still in a constant state of hardship and all I wanted to do was help others through my business. Why were other businesses prospering around me? Many endeavors that I witnessed were formulated with selfish motives and what I considered "get rich" schemes, and my entire business plan had been centered on making a difference. I had invested blood, sweat, and inestimable tears into the organization to no avail.

I plummeted into a state of fatigue. I contemplated what life would be like if I only remained focused on myself and my family. Would I be able to reenergize if I silenced my calling? During my wallow in self-pity, I gleaned a few key insights that would prove powerful enough for me to push through:

1. There is an abundance of resources available to us.
2. The flame within us has an infinite source of replenishment.
3. Oprah wasn't built in a day.

Each stone that had previously been in the way became a step. I made a conscious decision to adopt a relentless pursuit.

I recognized that I had the ability to make plans, but only God had the ability to make them come to fruition. Although I still experience fatigue, I will never quit, because I continuously humble myself to my purpose of building something that even I cannot conceptualize. I allow God to guide my hand a place every brick as I build a house that I have never seen the blueprint for, and I trust the process completely. I now know that I am not building alone nor am I responsible for the power and endurance needed to construct. Fatigue no longer lives here.

A Heroine in Heels: Vanessa Henderson

I met Vanessa at a book signing for a Consciously Beautiful Ambassador by the name of Dawn Angela. At the time, Dawn Angela was releasing her book *Timeless Rebel*. The atmosphere was filled with love and empowerment. I was seated next to some beautiful ladies whom I would come to adore: Shekina Farr Moore, CEO of Literacy Moguls, whose company was responsible for publishing Dawn Angela's book, and Vanessa Henderson, creator of The House of Van Miller. I was friends on Facebook with Vanessa, but we had never formally met.

Through general conversation with Vanessa, we instantly connected. She began to tell me about her heart condition. Vanessa was a household name, because her fashion and design house: The House of Van Miller and Van Miller International was responsible for clothing countless celebrities and even on the red carpet at the Emmys. The House of Van Miller was infamous in Atlanta for whimsical designs and elaborate pieces that reflected her extreme creativity but also the love for the empowerment of women. If you attended a fashion show, The House of Van Miller was certain to draw the "wow" factor. It was indisputable that Vanessa designed with her heart.

Prior to that day, Vanessa had been given the news that her heart was heavy. She was diagnosed with congestive heart failure. Emory Healthcare reports the following statistics:

- Nearly 5 million Americans are currently living with congestive heart failure (CHF).
- Approximately 550,000 new cases are diagnosed in the U.S. each year.[12]

The doctors concluded that Vanessa's heart could not keep up with her body, mind, spirit, and dream. Vanessa's weekly schedule included making appearances on red carpets, sketching and designing, delivering garments to photo shoots, and, the most strenuous of all, fashion shows. Her schedule was boisterous to say the least. The pace at which she was designing and toiling towards her dreams was not physically acceptable.

In a moment that seemed to have frozen amidst our conversation, she expressed many sentiments, but when speaking of her heart, I garnered fatigue to be among the most powerful.

There are times when your purpose outweighs any other factor. The calling is so deafening that you can't hear any other sound. Vanessa's calling to design clothes was planted as a child growing up amidst humble beginnings. Vanessa recalls, "We were the children who always had to wear other people's clothes." The irony of her evolving into the one who people seek to be clothed by is astounding. Vanessa's world would be shattered as she would later lose her mother to congestive heart failure. Upon receipt of Vanessa's diagnosis, caring family and friends would urge her to stop designing and return to her home. In response to this notion, Vanessa would say the most profound sentiment ever: "I can't allow my work to die." Her words pulverized my soul. When you work within your purpose, often you work to achieve a dream that no one else can see. It is sensible, because the vision was given only to you; however, your calling will not allow you to rest. Resting would be equivalent to death, and, for Vanessa, this simply was not an option. Life and abundance was on her horizon.

It wasn't until she began to shed layers of unproductive working relationships, her job, and unwanted emotional baggage that she received a favorable prognosis from her doctors.

In a little under six months, I watched her transform from fatigued to energized. So much so that when I invited her to be a featured designer in my first play *Lipstick Monologues*, she not only obliged but also designed a new line exclusively for the show, filled with seductive, sultry garments and pieces that did more for women's self-esteem in one minute than some designs do in centuries.

As time would pass, Vanessa would become one of my most trusted wardrobe designers and, most importantly, a beloved friend.

I saw her begin to work with more vigor and energy than many designers who had no health concerns. She was on the scene representing The House of Van Miller at red carpet events, plays, showcases, and, of course, fashion shows. The House of Van Miller continues to grow and flourish today. There is no doubt in my mind that the world will know Vanessa's work, because she demonstrates through her daily walk our ability to supersede exhaustion when we are driven by passion.

Vanessa owned it that night at the *Lipstick Monologues* and every other moment that life gives her. I will never forget the look on her face when I realized that she had turned fatigue into a force of power and that force would fuel her drive and determination.

With passion and purpose in the driver's seat, Vanessa hosts the Queen of Hearts Annual Tea and Fashion Show to create widespread awareness about heart disease and allow women to share stories in which others might find power, strength, and a system of support. During the Queen of Hearts Annual Tea, Vanessa showcases a line that she designs solely for the event. Each year, her event and love replenishes and grows. "I want women to learn to take care of their hearts and know the risks associated with heart failure, because we are wives and mothers and we have careers, but we often forget about ourselves," said Henderson.

I asked Vanessa if she had any plans to take a break to rest for her heart, and she replied, "I am unapologetic for working within my life's purpose, passion, and potential. I am a designer with purpose and for humanity. I won't ever rest." Vanessa's work will never die nor will her spirit; it will live indefinitely through her masterpiece affectionately called The House of Van Miller.

We are all plagued by fatigue. It seems as though "tired" is the new popular response when asked how we are doing. An abnormal response in today's society is, "I'm well rested." Why has "tired" become the new black?

Gone are the days that we take naps for leisure and seek balance in our lives. I, too, am guilty. For these reasons alone, we spend the majority of our lives in a constant state of fatigue. Many are on a quest to find our reason for existence, while others spend their days simply existing. This sad but true concept must be examined further if we truly want to soar with our greatest potential.

Here are some tips to beat fatigue:

- Listen to your body
  - Your body tells you when you need to slow down
- Let go of the notion that busy is the same as productive
- Make rest a priority
- Seek to achieve balance
- Disengage
  - Turn off the social media voices
- Exercise
- Eat
- Love

Look in the mirror with a truthful heart and ask yourself how you have benefited from being busy. What did you actually accomplish today?

If all you can come up with is that you posted on social media several times, sharing your every move, rant, and feeling, then you are diminishing your power.

AHIH Tip: A heroine in heels knows the value of her time and does not engage in activities that will absorb all of her resources or ensue fatigue.

While on a mission to save the world, among the greatest resources are time and energy. Many resources, such as money, material things, and even non-consumables like relationships, can be replenished, but time and energy often cannot.

Vanessa Henderson

I am not what has happened to me. I am stronger.

CHAPTER 10

Insecurity
in·se·cu·ri·ty
ˌinsəˈkyo͝orədē/
noun
"Uncertainty or anxiety about oneself; lack of confidence."[13]

> *"I will not be held hostage to what you speak of me.*
> *I am what I say that I am."*
>
> —Ardre Orie

The only sentiment scarier than fear itself is insecurity. It paralyzes us and holds us in unyielding bondage. From this emotion, we make the greatest, most impactful decisions in our lives that often haunt us for eternity. This single emotion revolutionizes our thought process and disables the very DNA that we have been given during supernatural conception.

Let's admit it: Insecurity is taboo and must be kept secret, locked, and hidden in the depths of our hearts. Most often, we deny access to the one person who can disrupt its negative impact and supersede its mission to kill and destroy: the one in the mirror.

We aren't even truthful with ourselves about the things that make us insecure.

Like most, I have and have maintained several insecurities throughout my life. I believe this to be a normal disposition. Let's first acknowledge that insecurities are okay. Our insecurities humanize us and make us recognize that, in our present state, we need assistance from the universe for the supernatural to occur. The messages that we receive tell so often and vividly the many reasons that we should not be insecure and teach us strategies to mask insecurities. In retrospect, this is completely wrong, because we are no longer sensitive to them and later become victim to decisions made from this state of insecurity that change the trajectory of our lives. Simply put, when we are insecure, we make bad decisions. These decisions affect the five major areas that determine the trajectory of our lives and the formula for our success: spirituality, finances, purity, education, and health. Let's explore further:

Spirituality

Our insecurities would have us believe that we are solely responsible for ourselves and that there is no presence of the supernatural, no access to miracles, and nothing greater to believe in.

Finances

Emotional spending is a byproduct of insecurity. When we make a decision to buy things out of a need to feel special, rewarded, or acknowledged in instances in which we cannot afford to do so, we feed our insecurities. Compromised decision making in this capacity leaves us at a deficit during life's most crucial moments with little to no room for advancement.

Purity

Insecurity is the value that we place on our lives. When we don't value ourselves enough to exercise restraint, we often give ourselves to people who are less than deserving. The reality becomes multiple sexual partners, unwanted pregnancies, financial hardships, emotional strife, and the exchange of energy that remains within our spirit for a lifetime. Giving of the absolute most valuable possession that we own needlessly is birthed out of insecurity.

Education

Through a state of insecurity, we tell ourselves that we don't need to learn more. "I already know that" are among the most dangerous words that we can speak. These words and this thought process removes our ability to grow. It is asphyxia of self. The other scenario is adopting fear associated with learning, growing, or leaving a comfort zone for fear of failure. This, in turn, is insecurity masked as excuses.

Health

Overeating and digesting things that are not respectful to our temples are secondary to insecurity. Not taking time to heal our souls from hurt is also a result of insecurity and the manifestation thereof.

    I discovered the root of my insecurities haphazardly. There was no great revelation or earth-shattering moment that revealed my truth. Instead, it graced me like a melody. I came to see vividly that my insecurity was rooted in rejection. This was my pain point. Throughout my life (prior to taking the leap of faith and resigning from my job), I played it safe. I only selected opportunities for growth that I was certain I could be good at or would obtain. I never took risks and walked through my life ensuring that my safety net was intact. This affected every area of my life from finances to relationships and even spirituality. I would not take risks, because they led me to face my insecurity of rejection.

Determining the source of your insecurity is one of the biggest power moves that you can make, because, when you clearly identify your pain point, it no longer has power over you. You learn how to respond to it and call it by name.

Upon my discovery, I penned a poem that I would later title: I Will Call You by Name.

I Will Call You by Name

Finally, I am brave enough to call you by name.

Not one single feeling seems to sting quite the same.

You find the most inopportune times to make your face clear,

but I am now wise enough to know

not to allow you the privilege of whispering in my ear.

At first glance, your mission appears to be rooted in the infliction of

hurt and unforgettable pain.

When you are near me, you bring back old memories

of worthlessness. You are the first cousin to shame.

When I was first introduced to you, I greeted you with a smile

and extended my hand. I thought that I knew how to receive you,

but no one ever becomes numb to your stain.

I wore you like a scarlet letter and your mist upon my face.

My smile turned to stone, and my heart hardened in absence of grace.

Knowing that you were near made me walk on glass.

I did not have armor of protection, and so my feet were shredded each time that you would pass.

Now your face is as clear as a sunlit sky and as bright as the moon.

I can see you coming in the distance.

I have prepared for you. I recognize you. I welcome you like tea in the afternoon.

For if you walk my way or whisper in my ear, this time I let you croon.

I can now softly hear you say, "I have something better in store coming your way."

I recognize you. You are not the evil force that I had once believed. You came like a thief in the night, but your mission was to save me.

I will never forget your face or your reflection. From now on, I will call you who you are. Your name is *rejection*.

I owe you an apology, I must admit. I welcome you in the distance and invite you in. You will be the one who saves my life. You will be the heroine.

I am no longer afraid of rejection because I realize that it allows me to get the best of what is in store for me as opposed to settling for what I think I want or need. Sometimes we dream too small and don't take time to imagine the absolute best life for ourselves, because our insecurities minimize our ability to conceive greater. In the end, we yield less harvest if we allow insecurities to take over, smothering every opportunity for abundance. I have befriended my insecurities, because I want to be on a first-name basis with them. I want them to understand me, and, most importantly, I want to understand them, for in that knowledge lies infinite power. In that knowledge, I am able to quiet the storm and position myself to be absolute, confident, and a visionary. I no longer question my self-worth, and I can now make every decision with a clean conscious, because I know just how valuable that I am. We all deserve this clarity. We all deserve to know how to tell our insecurities to sit down in the nearest corner while we pursue the best lives for ourselves, not simply because we deserve it but because we were created to live in abundance.

A Heroine in Heels: Elizabeth Clark

Friendship is the quickest way to expand your horizons.

—Ardre Orie

I met Elizabeth at my book signing for *Consciously Beautiful: I Am Enough*. I am convinced that I can feel the positive vibrations of others through social media, which is why I am so fond of it. We originally connected as I noticed her blog *Put on Your Big Girl Lipstick* (www.biggirllipstick.com). Not only did Elizabeth review cosmetics and share her love of beauty products, but there was also a subliminal message of self-love.

   I would later learn that Elizabeth was an educator and amongst what would appear to be a dying breed of those who share a love and luster for the education of our future (a girl after my own heart). Over time, I would grow to learn how much she cared for her students and wanted a better life for them.

   Elizabeth was raised in a two-parent home with inward and outward appearances of a traditional family with substantial core values and southern hospitality. I even became pen pals with her mother on Facebook and grew to love her messages of encouragement.

   As time and energy would reveal, Elizabeth and I were destined to be friends. Somewhere between hello and "I think that you are amazing," I revealed to Elizabeth that I had been a witness to domestic violence in my home as a child. She confided in me that she was the victim of domestic violence in her marriage. My heart broke, because I knew this sentiment all too well. Why Elizabeth? She was beautiful, educated, well traveled, reared in a two-parent home, and a good person to the core. How could this become a part of her story when she had been a witness to exactly how a man should treat a woman through one of the most astounding relationships: her parents?

The answer was simple. Insecurity.

Elizabeth and I met for coffee and had one of many heart-to-heart conversations, and she would reveal to me the source of her insecurity.

Let's be clear: We all have insecurities, and, whether we choose to admit it or not, our insecurities manifest in our actions. Elizabeth's insecurity manifested in loyalty. Elizabeth, like many women, took her wedding vows seriously. She believed that it was her job to fix anything that was wrong with her marriage. In her words, she was a "natural-born nurturer." Elizabeth's nurturing nature would later prove to be acceptance of verbal, emotional, and physical abuse.

Elizabeth not only fell victim to but also endured multiple mood swings and the emotional instability of her husband that led to comments from him like "I wish I never met you" and "You mean nothing to me."

Elizabeth recalls that she felt like she was living with a stranger at times. In the midst of her tumultuous relationship, Elizabeth would arrive at work upset and crying on several mornings, and, as countless women do, put on her "normal" face. The worst of the physical violence was on a normal drive to work in the morning in which a normal conversation resulted in Elizabeth being punched repeatedly in the leg closest to the driver's seat. "Strangely enough, he never hit me in my face." Elizabeth would later realize that her ex-husband recognized that bruises on her face would reveal to others the impact of his violence. What he had not recognized was that emotional scars and verbal abuse take form and leave powerful remnants of their presence as well.

There came a time when Elizabeth realized that she was responsible for her destiny, self-esteem, and insecurities and that she would also be held accountable for the decision to stay or leave. At any rate: "No victims allowed." Elizabeth notes that she had simply run out of emotion to give to the draining relationship. Elizabeth requested a divorce and had the strength to walk away with no children and her power that she would eventually rediscover.

Elizabeth is unquestionably a heroine in heels, because allowing me to share her story in this book marks the first time that she has decided to go public. She has told me on many occasions that she wants her story to be an inspiration to her students in teaching them to recognize signs of unhealthy relationships as well as to understand the importance of channeling your own strength to remove yourself from situations that are counterproductive to your personal growth and development.

To take it a step further, during our intimate talks, Elizabeth and I would make a conscious decision to do the work to recognize the root causes of our insecurities, a step that far too many of us skip or purposely overlook. I have learned that if we don't find the source, we will never cure the point of pain.

Elizabeth went on to share with me that, around age eight or nine, she was one of the first girls to reach a peak in height. This made her different. She began to make the simple comparisons that we all do to the other girls and spent a great deal of time agonizing over issues, such as height, weight, clothing size, and body shape. Elizabeth confided that she "can remember loathing [her] own body as early as third grade." Elizabeth made it clear that she received nothing but positive messages about her body and inner person in her home and from her parents, but her thoughts manifested in insecurities that created personal beliefs about who she was and what she was capable of.

Elizabeth also noted that a teacher of her physical education class would yell at her for being the slowest. From a young age, Elizabeth felt limitations on what she could do physically, and this teacher in particular fed the negative inner voice. Elizabeth notes that would receive instruction from this teacher over the course of five years and the significant impact that it had on how she saw herself. Ironically, Elizabeth teaches and empowers students to hear a positive inner voice that lacks limitations and instead creates hope and will power.

Even in the midst of Elizabeth's tumultuous relationship, she recognized the following two pieces of advice that were given to her by friends that helped get her through it:

1. Relationships are not supposed to be this hard. Elizabeth understood that true love doesn't repeatedly hurt so badly.
2. This is not the life that God has planned for you. When Elizabeth took into consideration her spiritual destiny, she quickly realized that God had never said in his word that he wished for her to travel through life under such circumstances.

While on a mission to get her power back, the following scripture appeared on several occasions for Elizabeth to fill her spirit with: "You intended to harm me, but God intended it for good to accomplish what is now being done, the saving of many lives" (Genesis 50:20).

Today, Elizabeth is powerful and has resolved to say goodbye to the shame that she associated with domestic violence. She is motivated by her faith in God and her students.

In her words, Elizabeth Clark is a faithful and loving daughter and friend, a dedicated teacher, and a woman who believes in the great plans that God has for her life.

I couldn't agree more.

Elizabeth Clark

The less we love and value ourselves as women, the more likely we are to allow people into our lives who also do not love and value us the way we should be.

CHAPTER 11

Sadness

Sadness

sad·ness
'sadnəs/
noun
"The condition or quality of being sad."[14]

Sadness is an unexplainable, suspended moment in time when we are forced to take off the mask and allow our wounds to heal.

—Ardre Orie

I remember it like it was yesterday. I had just given birth to my second daughter and for some reason felt that she would come to replace a family member. Some believe that souls within families recycle and the loss of a soul equals the birth of a new soul. Although I can't say this was my personal belief, for some reason the sentiment stuck in my mind.

My mother had been responsible for the care of my grandmother. My grandmother had recently had a surgical procedure and it was on the road to recovery.

One Saturday I awoke to a call from the rehabilitation center where my grandmother had been staying. This was not the first time that they had called me, so I was not alarmed. On this occasion, they did inform me that my grandmother had stopped breathing and had been transported to the local hospital. They did not specify if they had revived her; they only told me that they transported her to the hospital. I immediately contacted my mother to inform her as I knew that she would prepare to go to the hospital immediately.

Upon speaking to my mother, she did not sound alarmed either; we both know the importance of remaining calm. My grandmother had been through so many instances and she was one tough cookie to say the least.

I stayed on the phone with my mother until she reached the hospital.

When my mother arrived, the doctors asked to speak with her, so she told me she would call me back and hung up the phone. When she called back, she informed me that my grandmother had passed away. In disbelief, I asked my mother if she was certain.

This was real: my grandmother, the only grandmother whom I had known, the only blood-related support system that my mother and I had, was no longer alive.

I had no idea how to handle such a monumental time in my life and am forever thankful to my husband, because he showed me how to maneuver moments of sadness like these. He would help me to immediately recognize that I could not allow the sadness to overtake me as I had to be strong for my mother; she was an only child. Upon that time, I began to strategize and determine how I would assist my mother through this difficult time.

My husband helped me to pack our belongings, and we immediately hit the road to be with my mother in my hometown of Gainesville, Florida.

When we arrived, it was as if I was in a daze. There was no rhyme or reason to understand what had been happening.

Loss is among the most forceful catalysts of sadness. My grandmother had departed this life, and I never really got a chance to say goodbye. She would never meet my daughter London. I would never kiss or hug her again. I would never fill the void of emptiness that loss had brought to me.

Even today, I feel the least strong in the face of loss. As the years go by, I grow to understand that loss is a part of life. As the seasons change so shall life. Power is only harnessed when we live each moment as if it were the last, taking special care to transfer as much as possible to our loved ones and leaving pieces of ourselves behind. There is no expiration for life lived with purpose. The mist is infinite.

Four Seasons

I wish that I could have seen your face in summer. I wish that I could hold your hand in the rain. No one ever loved me and protected my heart. No one ever took the time to fuel the flame.

I wish that I could hold you closely in the fall. The leaves on the trees were the backdrop to our destiny, and life without you will never be the same.

I wish that I could kiss you deeply in winter. The warmth of your skin brought me a sense of wholeness from within. No one ever took the time to learn my heart. But you, my darling, you were after my soul; you wanted to love deeply from the start.

I wish that I could watch the rain with you in spring. Together we could have held hands and listened to the lovely melodies that the jay birds sing. A picnic in the park, an outdoor movie after dark—every moment with you was a gift. The weight of love so heavy laden that I never wanted it to lift.

But as the seasons pass, I sit in silence staring aloof into the glass, for I know that your face shall never grace mine again. You lived, you loved, and you taught me how to survive while lying in the hospital bed with no sign of life. I shall never forget when you took your last breath for an angel arrived with a summons of death.

I pray that Heaven has four seasons to reunite me with love.
I now release you to the stars above.

If only I could have seen your face in summer.

A Heroine in Heels: Yvonne Fry

The tenacious power that runs through every inch of Yvonne Fry is captivating. She has an ability to maneuver life with grace, poise, and a statuesque demeanor that can only be attributed to the acknowledgement of self-worth.

I would look to Yvonne periodically to fill my cup and speak words of wisdom into my soul because of the priceless knowledge that she had acquired along her journey but, more importantly, her innate ability to pour into another human being. She has this way of giving you immense information without batting an eye. She reminds me of ladies like Aretha Franklin who stand on stage and croon these amazing notes but stand as if they are leisurely singing in the shower, leaving everyone to ponder, "How did she just do that?"

I was introduced to Yvonne by an amazing educator named Tamethea Simmons, who had been instrumental in ensuring that my work to create and deliver services through the Pink Wish Foundation lived on in Tampa, Florida, even after I departed to live in Atlanta. Tamethea had suggested that we consider Yvonne as a guest speaker for our annual Pink Girls Rock spring brunch. Each year in May, I would host anywhere from 200–400 young ladies in a formal dining setting at the "members only" Tampa Club that overlooks the city of Tampa, Florida. There was always a beautiful assortment of young ladies ranging from those who had engaged in formal dining settings to those who had never been to a restaurant before. This event was the highlight of the time that we would spend teaching the young ladies etiquette and leadership skills. After learning of Ms. Fry and her amazing work, it was discernible that she would have an insurmountable amount of wisdom to share with our young ladies.

Her titles read like this:

- Fresh Picked Talent, Chief Entertainment Officer
- Fry Entertainment, Inc., Executive Producer
- Lines of Communication, President
- Mom (chauffer, cook, dry cleaner, scheduler, tutor, financier, psychiatrist, coach, civics teacher, spiritual leader, and ultimate responsible party)

And her list of affiliations read like this:

- Florida Commission on the Status of Women (FCSW), Chair
- Hillsborough Commission on the Status of Women (HCOSW), Chair
- Athena Society, Hospitality Chair
- The Spring of Tampa Bay, Advisory Board
- Plant City Chamber of Commerce, Governmental Affairs Chair
- Plant City Board of Adjustment
- Frameworks of Tampa Bay, Board Member
- Junior League of Tampa, Community Advisory Board Member
- Plant City High School PTSA, President
- Lincoln Elementary PTA, Membership Chair
- Working Women of Tampa Bay, member
- USF Women in Leadership and Philanthropy, member

I could end this chapter here, because Yvonne's luster for impactful living is self-explanatory. Notwithstanding, Yvonne's life would become a lighthouse beaconing strength in the midst of sadness.

Through our conversations and exchanges, I would learn that Yvonne's wisdom had not come as effortlessly as her delivery. Yvonne was raised on a farm and observed her mother and father toil. This is evident in her daily walk today, because, from outward appearances, one would think that she never sleeps. She is always attending events, to work, speak, make an appearance, and, most importantly, make a difference.

After her father departed from his earthly walk, Yvonne watched, aspired, and learned relentlessly from the two inevitable role models closest in her circle: her mother and her older sister.

When asked how she managed her sadness, she had the following to say:

"Understanding hurt, loss, and despair firsthand makes us far richer humans, able to relate to the realities others face. Losing my father at an early age gave me perspective and ultimately strength laced with compassion and patience. It still hurts, but it brings so much more with it that we can use towards a good purpose."

Yvonne learned to turn sadness into purposefulness. The resounding theme of her life sings, "There is work to be done." She exemplifies the "walk like you have somewhere important to go" sentiment, and she knows without question that she has several important tasks to complete, but, most importantly, she believes in her ability to do so. If we were brutally honest, we would acknowledge that there are several women who are superficially busy. Busy is the new black. However, how many are truly impacting the trajectory or course ahead for others?

Leading a life of impact and purpose comes with a hefty price tag. Yvonne revealed to me that in her early adulthood, she dealt with severe depression as well as physical issues. She would also share that she recognized the connection between mind, body, and spirit and acknowledges that, when one is affected, all are affected.

What helped Yvonne to triumph?

As a child, Yvonne's tutelage established through life on the farm would lead her to not only raise horses but also understand the process for breaking them. Yvonne carefully articulates that the process of breaking a horse begins with the horses standing tied. This revealed to Yvonne the power of understanding limitations and channeling strength in spite of them.

Moreover, Yvonne carefully notes that "God's provision and those who loved [her] even when it was really hard to" were instrumental in helping her unearth her purpose for living.

Today, Yvonne lives for her children. It is apparent through our interactions that her children are as important to her as the air that she breathes.

Yvonne learned from her parents that work had to be earnest and impactful. This lesson would later manifest when she watched her mother assume all of the same responsibilities that her father had once executed to keep the business and family afloat. Visions and subliminal coaching like this do not go unnoticed. Yvonne's mother had taught her through actions that sadness creates survivors.

Some would believe that sadness is permission to give up in the midst of life, but a heroine in heels recognizes this as the contrary. In addition to your life's mission, vision, and purpose, an encounter with sadness reveals what you will inevitably survive, creating the backdrop from which to empower those around you. For Yvonne, the amount of sadness that she experienced from the loss of her father was immeasurable, but her impact in the lives of others can be easily calculated. Her work, her pain, and her toil will never be in vain and will not return void.

"Finding purpose saved my life."

"To have something that you love more than yourself is reason for living."

Yvonne Fry

We get a lot of mixed messages about power and I see women and girls of all ages struggling with this concept. Power is defined as position or prestige. I challenge that notion. Power is actually at its height when one has an inspired vision that others can come alongside of and make a difference.

CHAPTER 12

Joy
joy
noun
"A feeling of great pleasure and happiness."[15]

Our work is at its highest value when it is done

for a cause, not applause.

—Ardre Orie

Joy is the sweetest scent I have ever known. It permeates the skin and flows from the soul. Joy can't be washed off or cleansed; it just lures.

When we discover that fragrance, we know it by name and bask in the certainty that no one can take it away.

Gwynnis Mosby is the embodiment of joy. Her reach has grown to know no boundaries. As the founder of the Gwynnis Mosby Academy of Makeup Artistry, she has taught countless students who have gone on to win Emmys and become makeup artists to every celebrity you can fathom. Of all of the lessons that she instills in the students under her close tutelage, the most valuable is joy.

Mrs. Mosby is known for treating all people the same, and she credits her father for this virtue. She watched countless examples in which his actions showed no favor. She recalls that he would often tell her, "You never know who you might meet." In the midst of a career spanning for twenty-nine years, celebrities and countless coveted professionals in the makeup and beauty industry, Mrs. Mosby, legend, icon, found me.

We were introduced by a lady, whom I have grown to love and who possessed the same joy that I speak of, named Eshe. Eshe, like many, had become a daughter to Mrs. Mosby and her husband, Pastor Phillip Mosby. Social media not only allowed me to connect with Eshe but also allowed her to see the toil and message behind the work of my cosmetics company I Love Me and the Consciously Beautiful Movement. Eshe was a two time Grammy Award winning singer, dancer and muse who had an extensive career filled with success. As people who thrive off of energy, Eshe and I connected. I would later learn that Eshe told Mrs. Mosby of my philanthropic endeavors and socially driven ventures as well as what she felt about my spirit. A year later, this connection would manifest in a personal call from Mrs. Mosby, legend, icon, stating that she wanted to honor me at her annual Le Maquillage Awards hosted during the PMAC Expo. The PMAC Expo was established by Mrs. Mosby as a way to honor the professionals who tirelessly work behind the scenes of entertainment's most acclaimed events. "I want to honor and appreciate the makeup and beauty professionals and bring forward those who are always behind the scenes," said Mosby. The PMAC Expo continues to experience exponential growth annually.

The call from Mrs. Mosby was a welcomed surprise, because she had touched me with her joy. As soon as I hung up the phone with her, I was ecstatic. About five minutes later, my human nature kicked in and heard a voice whisper, "You don't deserve that award."

I sat in silence with thoughts of calling Mrs. Mosby back to inform her that the award should go to someone other than me. Could it be possible that I had done enough to earn such an honor? What made me worthy of receiving an award from someone who had devoted so many years to the industry in which I was still quite new?

All of these questions clouded my judgment.

I must pause here and dissect this scenario, because it happens to all of us. I was afraid and insecure. We must learn to recognize these moments in our lives and be able to call them to the floor. Had I not had the strategies to deal with these feelings, I would have crumbled and missed one of the most confirming moments of my journey.

I would later speak with my friend and makeup artist Sebastian, who said "Girl, go and get your award." From that moment on, I told the little voice and leader of the negative committee in my head to sit down and be quiet. With my dignity back intact, I was contacted by Sheldon Horton, an amazing makeup artist and hairstylist, who was one of the professionals who worked diligently to put the Le Maquillage Awards together. He not only congratulated me but also commended me on the work that I had done. His call was also reassuring that I deserved to be exactly where God had placed me. Sheldon requested that I send him documentation of my work including videos, press releases, pictures, etc. My confirmation was further established. I had more than enough to send him. I had so much documentation of all of the things that I was working on that I had to sort through it all and decide what to send. As I went through the last five years of my work, I felt a sense of joy. No one could question the work that I had put in. The sleepless nights, countless hours of trying to learn about an industry that I knew nothing about, and, most of all, the love. No one could question my work or my worth, not even me. Needless to say, the awards ceremony was amazing and marked one of the proudest moments of my life. When I stood to give my acceptance speech, I did so with conviction, because I knew that I deserved to be there. I was overcome with joy that I had waited for so long to be recognized, not by others but by myself. I sat in awe and soaked in the moment. This was the first time in my entire life that I said the words "well done" to myself. The joy was abundant, infinite, a sweet fragrance that I shall never forget.

I'd like to share my acceptance speech from this joyous day with you:

> Giving honor to God for the gift of breath and vision. I honor Queen Gwynnis Mosby for recognizing the unsung heroes.
>
> To my husband who supports me through everything, and my children who love me unconditionally, I honor you.
>
> And to my mother who told me that I could do anything, you are my heartbeat.
>
> My life's mission is to teach people how to turn their insecurities into fuel.
>
> The Bible tells us that the root of all evil is money. I agree, but I also believe that the root of evil is fear and insecurity.
>
> I got into this industry because I was tired of the media and magazines making everyday women feel like they did not measure up.
>
> Fear and insecurity makes us feel like we are not enough.
>
> Far too many times we don't feel pretty enough, small enough, tall enough, smart enough and wealthy

enough, don't have enough clients and God forbid enough makeup!

What I know is that we were all created in a perfect image, so, as long as we are in a constant state of becoming the best versions of ourselves, we are enough.

Lastly, I met a man who worked his makeup brushes so well that I retired mine. Sebastian has become my business partner and friend, and, together, we are making over as any women as our time will allow us through these programs.

I have a goal to makeover 500 women and teen girls this year. I don't know how, but God does.

We need people to join us, makeup artists and business partners, people to help us create awareness about this movement, because every person deserves to know that the reflection in the mirror is enough.

Someone is out there right now feeling like they are not enough. I am here to encourage you. I am here to let you know that you will make it in spite of your circumstance. Don't give up. Keep going. You are enough.

Although I've said a lot, I beg of you to remember one thing.

Say it with me: I *am* and that's enough.

Thank you so much!

God bless you all.

A Heroine in Heels: Gwynnis Mosby

"I've been working in this industry for twenty-seven years, and I've never received an award. The makeup artists that I have trained have won Emmys and all sorts of awards, but this is my first."

—Gwynnis Mosby after receiving the first "Legend Award" during the 2014 PMAC Expo.

The highest honor is to be awarded by those who truly know you. The joy is indescribable. I had the honor of witnessing Mrs. Mosby surprised and in shock to receive what would be one of her highest achievements from the people that knew her best.

Gwynnis Mosby, legendary Atlanta-based celebrity makeup icon and founder of the Gwynnis Mosby Makeup Academy, has dedicated over two decades to the industry with a career spanning over twenty-nine years. Mrs. Mosby created beautiful faces for celebrities like Usher, Toni Braxton, Tupac, Faith Evans, and TLC just to name a few. Of all of her accomplishments, the one that I found to be most intriguing was her joy.

I had the privilege to sit at the feet of Mrs. Mosby and allow myself to be enveloped in her joy. When asked what drives her, she replied, "I am driven everyday by my Lord and Savior Jesus Christ. He is always first. I simply love what I do." Mrs. Mosby explained that she loves her work so much that her energy levels grow as the hours pass. "I can easily work all day and into the morning. By three or four a.m., I am just getting started." She expressed to me that every time she does makeup, she is happy to be able to do what she loves.

Mrs. Mosby grew up in a close knit family with brothers and sisters who believed in being there for one another. Mrs. Mosby recalls that her siblings were among her best friends. "Although I loved having friends, I never needed friends, because I had family." That same sense of pride and loyalty would extend to her high school sweetheart who became her husband, best friend, and trusted confidant. Pastor Phillip Mosby embodies the same contagious joy which draws people near and into their world. Together, they built a growing empire with a legacy that will not soon be forgotten.

After high school, Mrs. Mosby began her collegiate career in pursuit of a degree in education. While in college, she attained a job working in the pharmaceutical department of a local drugstore. In this capacity, she acquired a background and understanding of chemicals. "You never quite realize how God is preparing you for all that he has in store for you," said Mrs. Mosby. "I used to make fun of my sister when she would put on makeup and often told her that she looked ridiculous."

At age nineteen, Mrs. Mosby decided that she would indulge and try makeup for herself. She allowed her makeup to be done at a makeup counter by a then budding company called Fashion Fair. During the '80s, color was in! As the makeup was being applied, the makeup artist told Mrs. Mosby that when she turned her around to face the mirror, she would be in for an amazing surprise, and boy was she. Mrs. Mosby was so appalled by the makeup that she screamed. The makeup artist probably assumed that she screamed in excitement, but I digress. From that moment on, Mrs. Mosby deemed that makeup was not for her. She wore minimal. As she continued her career at the pharmacy, a lady who relentlessly sold goods for a cosmetics company named Chambray, made regular visits to the pharmacy and to Mrs. Mosby. She would eventually convince Mrs. Mosby to work with the company and learn about their products, which would be carried in the pharmacy. Mrs. Mosby's product knowledge was extensive, and the pharmacy owners would determine that her talents would best be suited in the cosmetics department. This would be a pivotal moment in the manifestation of God's greater plan in her life.

Mrs. Mosby was a natural when it came to explaining products and demonstrating product use. Mrs. Mosby's sister-in-law had also recently became a sales rep for a company named Mary Kay that would revolutionize the beauty and makeup industry. During a home party, she would instruct Mrs. Mosby how to apply the makeup to her face, and, in that moment, Mrs. Mosby fell in love with the concept as well at the natural look of the beauty as opposed to the over indulgence in color. This sentiment still rings true today as Mrs. Mosby's applications are flawless. Her clients look like the best versions of themselves as opposed to another person completely after makeup application.

Her knowledge continued to grow, and during her junior year, Mrs. Mosby made the decision to resign from college and accept a new position as the head of the southeast region cosmetics department for Treasury Drug, which was a subsidiary of J.C. Penney. In accepting the job, she was told that she would be required to travel for several weeks out of the year. The job was also monumental in nature as she would be the first African-American to be appointed into the position. With a two-month-old daughter at the top of her list of priorities, she and her husband had to make the tough decision to either accept or decline the position. In true Mosby fashion, they put their heads together and determined to put family first. In doing so, Mrs. Mosby was given another position in the company overseeing the catalog department. A major component of her new job was the completion of a tremendous amount of paperwork. Mrs. Mosby found herself in the midst of a crossroads when she was informed that she could either embark upon a career path of constant travel or move to Pittsburgh. God continued to speak to her, and she knew that there was a greater calling on her life that did not include the options presented. Mr. and Mrs. Mosby prayerfully made the decision for her to quit her job. After she had done so, her then boss walked her to her car and spoke these words over her life: "You will never be anything." He was referring not only to her declining the monumental job offer but also to her resigning from college during her junior year. Mrs. Mosby decried that time in her life but what was most astonishing were these words: "Any time that you take a leap of faith when God tells you to, he will always make a way."

The tree of life that God was planting for Mrs. Mosby would begin to grow branches when a girlfriend who was a makeup artist asked Mrs. Mosby if she wanted to ride with her to her cosmetology school. While there, Mrs. Mosby would find her way to the esthetician certification department. Upon inquiry, she was informed that in order to do makeup, she would have to obtain her certification as a licensed esthetician. Mrs. Mosby enrolled on the spot and began active pursuit of what would become her legacy.

Mrs. Mosby was one of the few African-Americans enrolled at her school. In addition to her coursework for her certification, she would continue to hone her skills as a makeup artist. "I would do makeup anywhere. I knew that I had to build a credible reputation and a name for myself," says Mrs. Mosby. Upon working at a local fashion show, she noticed that the African-American models were not happy with their makeup as done by makeup artists from various ethnicities. She recalled that one model went to the bathroom and cried after seeing her makeup, because she looked green. In an effort to make a difference, Mrs. Mosby approached the director of the show and requested to do all of the faces of the women of color. "I requested to do makeup for all of the African-Americans, Asians and Hispanics, because I knew exactly what they needed to look their best." Mrs. Mosby toiled relentlessly. She would go on to explain that her first year of working was solely for free. She worked with a photographer for one year with no pay but the promise of a bright future. "I built a solid portfolio that showed my body of work and skill set, and I learned the proper application for makeup for various types of photography." During Mrs. Mosby's second and third years of working, she began to break even. Upon her fourth year, she saw more financial gains and even turned a profit. Her fifth year would prove to be prodigious as she retired her husband from his job to become her agent. Twenty-nine years, later, Pastor Phillip Mosby is still her agent.

The common threads in Mrs. Mosby's lineage are linked by joy—the joy that she shared for her family and her work—and the integrity that has enabled her to scale the greatest heights of the profession.

As her reputation grew, she began to receive invitations from celebrities to go on tour and provide her services. Her level of integrity and the "treat everyone the same" disposition that her father had instilled would prove to be among her most valuable characteristics. While on tour with Toni Braxton, she was asked what her favorite song by Toni was, and she replied, "I haven't heard any of them, but I am sure that I will get to hear all of them, while we are on tour." Mrs. Mosby was never star-struck and never glorified any specific person, only God. This allowed her to become so sought after that she had to find a way to provide her services to her clients even when she was booked to capacity. Thus, the manifestation of the Gwynnis Mosby Makeup Academy (GMMA). GMMA was established from a need to ensure that the profession lives on with quality education of techniques and proper application with integrity at the forefront. Today, Mrs. Mosby can be found teaching the best and brightest emerging talent in the makeup and beauty industry. Mrs. Mosby's list of students include Sheryl Thomas, the first African-American to be appointed as the Head Makeup Supervisor for Disney on Broadway; D'Andre Michael, makeup artist and photographer for celebrities, including Mary J. Blige and Garcelle Beauvais; Nyssa Green, five-time Emmy award winning makeup artist; and my friend and international makeup artist Sebastian. For every life that she touches, there is a glimmer of joy that can never be forgotten.

Along the way, she has taken time to nurture the many valuable relationships in her life, especially her relationship with God. Because of her commitment to her spirituality, she will forever be able to spread the sweet scent of joy to every person that she encounters. Mrs. Mosby realizes that the joy she experiences was never given to her by the world and that the world cannot take it away. Mrs. Mosby is a heroine in heels.

Gwynnis Mosby

Whether you realize it or not, God is always preparing you for the future and what he has in store for you.

CHAPTER 13

Grace
grās/
noun
"Simple elegance or refinement of movement."[16]
Favor
Approval

Some say that they have come this far by faith. I say that I've come this far by both faith and grace. The presence of faith is an open door for the presence of grace and truth be told, I can't live without either.

—Ardre Orie

In Christian beliefs, grace is defined as the free and unmerited favor of God as manifested in the salvation of sinners and the bestowal of blessings.

Grace will take you places that talent cannot. Although I have worked for every blessing, grace has carried me along the way. I am reminded of the lyrics of one of my favorite gospel songs, "Take My Hand, Precious Lord" written by Thomas Dorsey.

These powerful lyrics were sung by gospel icons like Mahalia Jackson and Elvis Presley. "Take My Hand, Precious Lord" was also said to be a favorite hymn of Reverend Dr. Martin Luther King Jr.

What I found to be the most interesting is the story behind the lyrics. As a writer, I am always intrigued by the sentiment in which something was written. My research gleaned that the composer, Dorsey, who had left a life as a jazz musician to become a pastor, was in church on a Sunday when he received a telegram that his wife had passed away shortly after giving birth to their child. He would later learn that his newborn baby passed away also.

How could anyone endure?

Approximately a week later, he was sitting at his piano and began composing the lyrics to what I recognize as one of the most powerful songs ever. What Thomas Dorsey was searching for is essentially what each of us search for night and day: the strength to go on. Whether in times of happiness or great despair and whether we realize it or not, we search for anything that can help us in our daily walks.

Grace is walking fearlessly in the fog of the unknown. Grace is the magic carpet that floats beneath your feet when you are unable to take the first step. It is the wind beneath our wings.

Grace makes people say, "How does she do it?"

The ability to demonstrate graciousness is long remembered. The acknowledgment of grace and gracious behaviors sets one apart in a crowd. In my humble opinion, the opposite of grace is entitlement.

I believe that we should all walk with expectancy of the energy that we place into the world. We should all walk in expectation of the manifestation of the work that we have put into motion, but entitlement is the contrary.

We harness the most power when we show gratitude for the effort, resources, and gifts that others sow into our lives. These things are not guaranteed. There is nothing more power draining than a sense of entitlement. This pattern of thought is a surefire way to crash and burn. I have come to realize that people enjoy giving to those who have a sense of appreciation and recognize the efforts taken to do so.

She who demonstrates grace holds the power of resilience when walking towards the light of destiny.

Grace will lead me on.

I believe that our true character can be revealed through grace. It is unmerited but gives each of us power beyond measure. When we recognize that not one single moment is owed to us and that each second we are allowed to breathe, smile, and exist, we acknowledge grace.

Grace will lead me on.

A Heroine in Heels: Monica Wright

It still baffles me that the biggest personas have the most gracious spirits. In a time where selfies and vain agendas are served up freshly and fiercely, humans like Monica Wright grace our presence, giving life and light a new disposition. Monica, a fusion of humility and confidence, is grace personified.

Selected second overall by the Minnesota Lynx in the 2010 WNBA Entry Draft, Monica is a bona fide star! Since being drafted, Monica's work resulted in her becoming a two-time WNBA champion.

Monica is not only beautiful, but also her spirit is infectious. I was introduced to Monica by her cousin Dynasty Tennison, who is a producer on my first documentary currently in production, entitled: *I AM*. Dynasty recognized that Monica would be an excellent fit for the documentary, because our purpose is to highlight ladies who knew their own strength and could provide invaluable pillars of advice for women and girls to increase their self-perception and self-worth. We went through the normal process of solicitation and pre-interview, and the detail that stood out the most about Monica was her grace. Throughout the entire process, she expressed her gratitude for the opportunity to empower women by participating in a project in which she is passionate about. Let's be clear: she did not have to be gracious. We are talking about Monica Wright. If you don't know who she is, google her! Her work on the court speaks for itself. Further, her game off the court is equally impressive.

How could Monica maintain such a sense of humility? What allowed her to be so effortlessly graceful?

From my observations, Monica's grace walked courageously before her because of two key factors:

1. She understood her purpose.
2. She saw her purpose as a developing body of work.

So often, we rush to find our purpose and get lost, because we fail to realize that it is a journey. Monica expressed her sentiments on her life's purpose: "I feel that my purpose in life up to this point is to use basketball as my platform and vehicle to glorify God and to empower, mentor, and encourage others."

Monica attributes the many successes and failures of her childhood to her solid grounding today. A tremendous part of who she has become is her mother and father whom she recognizes proudly for raising both her and her brother with a strong sense of morality. It is most apparent to those who are in Monica's presence that her grace extends beyond good teaching. She is of good character. Her demonstration of sportsmanship and loyalty to her profession alone is commendable.

It is compulsory that ladies like Monica Wright are recognized and honored for women and girls of all ages to aspire to. In a world filled with mixed messages about how women must be petty, use their bodies, and step on the prosperity of others to get ahead, Monica is the polar opposite. She is a true testament to the power that grace will lead you to do exactly what you have been placed here to do if you allow yourself to be used for the higher purpose and benefit of making a positive impact in the lives of others. Monica is a vessel.

In spite of Monica's grace, she recognizes that without her relationship with God, she no longer thrives with a powerful disposition: "When I try to do things with my own strength and lose sight of God, I often make mistakes."

As women, we all make mistakes and often out of insecurities. Monica recognized a correlation between her early involvement in sports and her self-esteem and self-worth. Monica urges women and girls to love their imperfection: "We must learn to love our imperfections and embrace [them] just as much as we do the things that we most like about ourselves."

There are so many misconceptions and stereotypes about ladies who play sports. I asked Monica, if she could change any misconceptions, which would she choose to educate the masses about and why? "I would change the perception that women in sports are overly aggressive. It is possible to be a strong female athlete and still be tenderhearted and compassionate. I feel that those characteristics exemplify strength over physical ability."

Through our time together, I know Monica is indeed tenderhearted and compassionate. We joked about working out together, and I told her that I did not wish to die, just engage in a good workout. In true Monica Wright fashion, she replied, "It's just great that you want to take care of yourself." She sees the best in herself and others. It is why she is here and her reason for existence. This supernatural assignment will transcend Monica as she gracefully lets her light shine as a beacon of hope for all of those watching.

Here's the best piece of advice that Monica shared with me, which I will continue to share with others that their light might never become dull: "All women should know not to compromise who they are or what they were created to do for anyone." Monica notes that this can often be a struggle for women, because "we all want to be married one day." Monica has shown the world exactly how not to compromise and that grace will always lead us on.

Grace touches your spirit when you encounter it. It is not easily forgotten. In my humble opinion, the gracious inherit the true riches of the earth. Monica Wright is grace personified.

Monica Wright

I learned long ago that it was unrealistic to compare myself to people who don't do what I do on a daily basis.

CHAPTER 14

Desire

Desire

de·sire
dəˈzī(ə)r/
noun
"A strong feeling of wanting to have something or wishing for something to happen."[17]

Faith
Fear
Fantasy

As the soul yearns, so shall the universe conspire.
—Ardre Orie

A Dance with Death

I have always used writing as a tool to heal from within. It provides opportunities for reflection and insight to your innermost thoughts and the sentiments of your heart. Upon discovering a lump in my breast for the third time, I wrote the following blog post that speaks to the very heart of desire:

If someone asks you what you want, there are myriad things that come to mind. However, when you are staring at the face of death, your true desires are revealed.

I rarely speak on extreme personal issues, because I was raised to be proud and never share too many intricate details since it is simply nobody's business. For some reason, life keeps showing me that sometimes our darkest moments are everybody's business.

I spend much of my time pouring what I feel to be positive energy into the world from any medium permitted, and then there are those moments that I have to go back and read my own quotes, digest my own blogs, and watch my own media, because I need encouragement to endure.

Today, marks the third time that I dance with death. Although it sounds harsh, it is the honest truth.

About a week ago, I discovered for the third time a lump in my breast. The time period between the moment of discovery and the initial doctor's visit is absolutely agonizing.

This is the moment that the needle hits the record and the music begins.

The melody begins slowly and the sound of classical strings fill your heart and mind. Your listening ear becomes keen as the notes appear as the faces of the people that you love the most. Your eyes fill with tears as you consider that you might not have an opportunity to spend the "couple of forevers" that Chrisette Michele sings so beautifully about with your husband. The notion that the infinite heartbeat that yearns inside of you for your children may cease to exist is absolutely deafening. Tears roll down your face as you are summoned to the dance floor. To dance with death is to dance with desire.

For people like me who thrive off of music, an invitation to the dance floor is always an honor but not when you dance with your mortality.

The Bible tells us to be confident in the unknown, for the creator holds the key to life's myriad experiences and the meanings that accompany them, but, in our flesh, we often submit to the inner voice that tangos with uncertainty when the music begins. To dance with death is to dance with desire.

The strum of the guitar leads you to a familiar melody that brings you peace. It is desire.

The melodies of my heart accompanied by lyrics of love speak my desires. "I desire to live" is the loudest, sweetest music to my ears. I desire to serve God and love my husband. I desire to raise my children and give them the comfort that resides in knowing without question that they are loved and worthy of love. I desire to be a good daughter and friend. I desire to fulfill my purpose on earth and share my gifts. I desire to live.

When you dance with death, there is no greater sound that fills your core than the resounding lyrics "I desire to live." And although I know not what the future holds, I rest assured that there are too many women and men who have been called to the dance floor to two step with the possibility and often reality of breast cancer. When will the music end?

My first invitation to dance was extended when I was in high school at the age of sixteen. Back then, this topic was taboo to say the least. No one adult or of a similar age had spoken of discovering lumps in their breast. This was even before the massive movement chartered by Susan G. Komen to paint the nation pink. I was alone on the dance floor with death. I had no one to talk to and no one who understood. I underwent surgery to remove it and was told that it was benign. I returned to school and never spoke of it. I was embarrassed. I did not learn much from that experience except the reinforcement of my sentiments to remain silent about personal issues.

Fast forward fifteen years, and I received another invitation. This time, I was pregnant with my first daughter Lauren, and now, I considered the alternative. Death had grabbed my hand. What if I would die and never have an opportunity to raise my daughter? What if I left behind my new husband? The melody was melancholy and absolutely morbid.

Several months after giving birth, I underwent another surgery to remove another benign tumor. The words "you are okay" dwelled in my heart like an infinite vibration. The song ended, and death had let go of my hand.

Since that time, I have learned to not be ashamed of the scars that I bear on my chest and dance daily with multiple partners. I dance with prayer, peace, happiness, hope, and, most importantly, love. I have learned to live each day as though it could be my last. I have learned to seize the moment and create lasting pieces of myself like crazy. I desire to leave my talents here on earth as God intended.

I can only pray that this dance that I now face ends with the same finale as the last two songs. Throughout my dances with death, my desires have been revealed. I thought that I wanted fortune. I thought that I wanted to build an empire. I thought that I wanted to be a mogul. But my dance with death revealed that my innermost desire is to live and love. Those are the words that death whispers to me as we dance.

I am reminded of my absolute favorite song "I Hope You Dance," written by Lee Ann Womack. This song is a constant reminder to each of us to live each day with rigor and relevance.

As I move closer to the dance floor and embrace the melody, I feel stronger than ever. I understand with gratitude that I was placed here to be of service, and, unless I am grounded in this notion, I will always misstep on the heels of death. I can't say with certainty what tomorrow holds, but I've learned to dance quite well. I hope you dance.

A Dance in the Darkness

I dance with you in the darkness. I dance with you in my dreams. Until I meet you face to face, nothing is what it seems.

I can hear you beckoning for me in the distance. I beg of you to draw me near. You know the depths of my soul and the intensity of my fear.

If I cannot catch a glimpse of your shimmer or touch the hemline of your cloak, my life will cease to move forward and sadness will convoke.

When the smoke and mirrors clear, there is nothing left to say. I am dancing with desire, the perfect end to my day.

I dance with you in the darkness. I dance with you in my dreams. Until I meet you face to face, nothing is what it seems.

I am dancing with desire. It was all but a dream.

When an ordinary person finds the strength to overcome obstacles and create an extraordinary life, she is a heroine.
—Ardre Orie

A Heroine in Heels: Lovilla Santiago

I was introduced to Lovilla, or Love as we affectionately call her, by my friend and makeup artist Sebastian. He was the link in a connection that would become more than just a friendship but a bond. I told Sebastian that I was looking for a model who had attained success in the industry with a compelling story to tell. Before I could even finish my sentence, he said, "Say no more. Lovilla." I had seen her work. The word "amazing" does very little to describe her range of talent as a model. Lovilla, a highly sought after international model, could transform into every culture and element of fashion that a designer could ever want, need, or imagine. She was a photographer's dream. An opportunity to shoot Lovilla was an opportunity to transform your portfolio from amazing to astounding.

After Sebastian informed Lovilla of my desire to work together, she became excited as she too had been following my work with my first book *Consciously Beautiful: I Am Enough*. What I know for certain is that iron sharpens iron, and positive energy always finds a way to connect with positive energy. The connection between Lovilla and I would later produce a collaboration that we both felt extremely passionate about. Together, we would decide to write her memoir.

Lovilla grew up in the Philippines in an immensely humble environment. The farm in which she and her family lived had no electricity. Each day for three years, Lovilla would walk twelve miles to school. Her miles would fall upon the only pair of shoes that she owned at that time. Lovilla recalls not having a TV in her home and standing outside of neighbors' homes to peer through their windows to watch their TVs. At times, she would be met with children inside the home yelling at her, "Hey, you are not supposed to be watching TV." On other instances, some children would be nice enough to invite her in. As the only girl and youngest of six brothers, Lovilla's mother chose her name because she knew that there was something special about her. Even in the midst of having no electricity, Lovilla saw beyond her circumstance, the first indication of a heroine in heels. Lovilla knew that with dedication and hard work she could transform her life into one that would create better circumstances for herself and her family.

In the midst of Lovilla pouring out her heart to me about her family, we were both overcome with emotion. We cried over the phone for at least an hour. It was absolutely transparent that she believed in her inner voice, innate power, and the circulation of positive energy.

In so many instances, girls are born into circumstances that seem to nurture failure. Lovilla turned every scenario into a stepping stone to foster progress and drive her success.

How had she managed to overcome her circumstance?

What did she desire that led her to nurture a vision of success?

Today, Lovilla's desires are easily recognizable to those that know her. In her words: "I want to work and make money to help my family." Everything that she does is for her family. You often hear people speak of this, but her actions tell the true story.

After moving to the United States, Lovilla was so driven to embark upon her modeling career that she began to take self-timed photos with a camera mounted on a tripod. She was discovered by someone who thought that the photos were amazing. Her ability to transform and knowledge of her body and angles was incomparable. A year after Lovilla moved to the United States, she would learn of her brother's illness. She began booking modeling jobs and earned money to send to her brother to assist with medical bills. She would later lose her brother and assume a great deal of the financial responsibility for the care of his children. In an emotional plea, Lovilla promised her mother and father that she would buy them a home. She made this promise because she believed in her ability to work with dignity and intensity that would help her keep her promise. In the midst of her toil, she would learn that her father had passed away. Although he never saw the home, Lovilla kept her words pure and true and had a house built to honor her mother and father.

Lovilla credits her husband of many years for the continuous support of her career and goal to help her family.

Lovilla arrived in the United States with a dream of becoming a model. Today, Lovilla is one of the most sought after models who has graced countless magazine covers, worked with numerous photographers, represented a multitude of brands, and now mentores a plethora of aspiring models.

Aspiring and seasoned models approach Lovilla daily asking for advice and connections. In an industry that is often revered for obloquy, Lovilla shares all of her knowledge in hopes that other models will prosper. "I've been blessed, so I truly just want to help others. There is enough in this world for all of us if we are willing work hard."

Lovilla's desire to disregard the limitations placed upon her life catapulted her career and destiny. Among all of her hopes and dreams, her desire to ensure that her work results in her family living the best life possible is the top priority at which she succeeds every day.

When our greatest desire is to make a positive difference in the lives of others, the universe will conspire to bring our desires to fruition. Lovilla is the manifestation of desire.

Lovilla Santiago

"The hardships that I experienced helped me value what I have now."

Conclusion

The most important skill set that we can acquire is the ability to harness our innate power to save ourselves. The second most important skill set that we can acquire is the ability to harness our innate power to save others. I once read that the mind was a beautiful servant and a dangerous master. A heroine in heels understands the significant correlation between the mind and her use of her emotions. If we are able to master our thoughts, we gain access to the power box that holds all of the controls to our emotions.

Whether we have been victimized, abused, left, beaten, forgotten about, hurt, bound or broken, the disposition in which we see ourselves and the synergistic power of our choice of emotions will determine the outcome.

Newton's third law of motion states: "When one body exerts a force on a second body, the second body simultaneously exerts a force equal in magnitude and opposite in direction on the first body."[18]

This law is applicable to life as we are in a constant state of receipt of forces upon our bodies, lives and minds. The greater question becomes: What force will we exert in opposite direction of the first body of force? Simply put, what will our response be to life's occurrences? This will determine our level of success.

We must prepare for infinite greatness and the presence of abundance in our lives. We must expect it. We must walk fearlessly into our destinies with no regard for failure or the factors that threaten our happiness or success. We have the power to do all of these things and more if only we believe.

The essence of the woman is to nurture, protect, and give life. Unless self-imposed, there are no boundaries that can contain the inherent power that fills every molecule that forms our existence.

I have chosen to see myself as powerful instead of a fatherless child or a woman not worthy of love. I have chosen to see myself as powerful enough to resign from a safe career and skydive with no wings into a life of work I could have only dreamed of. I know that without God and my spiritual connection, none of this would be possible nor would I be able to envision my life differently. I understand the infinite greatness that we each possess, and I choose to tap into that power daily. From this day forward, I will never allow anything to debase my value or worth. I am not a victim. I resolve to be the heroine of my own life. Will you resolve to be the heroine of yours?

It is my personal mission to ensure that every woman and girl who touches this book seeks to discover the power that rests, rules and abides within us. To this end, I have established the Consciously Beautiful Movement, an active extension of this book.

The Consciously Beautiful Movement exists to empower women and girls to love the reflection they see in the mirror and demystify and deconstruct media messages that demean women. If several people were asked to ponder their ideas and notions of beauty, it is certain that there would be variations and differences of opinion as every eye has been cultured to see beauty from his or her vantage point. Subsequently, acts of kindness, such as volunteering to uplift one's community, lending a helping hand to those in need, or even making a loved one smile, would all be classified as beautiful no matter who you ask. Thus, although not glorified and saturated in the media, true beauty resides in the heart of those that make the world a better place to be.

The Consciously Beautiful Movement hosts the following activities annually to empower women and girls in the US as well as beyond our borders:

CB Book Talk Tour

Multi-city tour with Author Ardre Orie sharing the messages of triumph and self-discovery with intimate groups of readers and audiences.

CB Empowerment Sessions

The focus for all CB Empowerment Sessions is teaching women and girls to recognize and demystify harmful media messages and inaccurate portrayals that degrade the value of women and girls. Attendees leave with an increased awareness of media tactics and strategies to filter messages for self-sustainability.

CB Mental Health Consortium

The CB Mental Health Consortium is a network of mental health professionals and resources that assist in the provision of women's and girls' use and knowledge of effective strategies to increase self-acceptance and maintain healthy lifestyle practices to thrive.

CB Annual Heart 2 Heart Retreat

The CB Annual Heart 2 Heart Retreat encourages openness and authenticity and allows women to engage in activities to acknowledge, understand, and love the reflection that they see in the mirror.

Pink Wish Academy

In partnership with the Pink Wish Foundation (www.pinkwish-foundation.org), the Consciously Beautiful in Pink program offers self-esteem building programs for schools, church groups, and local community groups utilizing modules to increase the self-esteem and decision making process for young ladies. This program was established for young ladies ages eight through fourteen.

***I AM*, the Documentary**

I AM is an American documentary film executive produced by Ardre Orie. The film candidly documents one woman's mission to expose the myriad of factors that contribute to the downward spiral of self-esteem in women and girls that affects all facets of life ranging from education to the acceptance of behaviors that often result in self-destruction.

I AM interweaves stories of real women and teen girls with candid interviews from esteemed professionals from a myriad of industries who reveal the societal impact on the way that we define beauty and self-worth.

The film's resounding message "I AM" is purposed to ensure that every viewer recognizes themselves as enough and is critical at every stage of life.

CB Ambassadors Program

Established for teen girls and women in multiple cities in the US as well as internationally, CB Ambassadors are those who desire to make a difference in their communities by hosting two Consciously Beautiful Empowerment Sessions using the CB curriculum provided as well as making appearances in their city at events that are created to empower women. CB Ambassadors are models for the Consciously Beautiful Movement and spread the Consciously Beautiful message through social media and their networks.

It is my hope that you, the reader, will join me in this mission by sharing this valuable work with the women and girls in your lives. There is an uncanny sense of freedom that comes with self-acceptance and knowledge of self-worth. I want every woman and every girl of every age to rise in the morning, look in the mirror, and say *"I am enough,"* knowing without question that they have every ounce of power that they will ever need.

A Heroine in Heels Mantra

I will honor my innate power.

I renounce failure.

I will remain diligent in my work.

I renounce fatigue and complacency.

I will hasten towards the abundance that awaits me.

I will seek happiness and joy in the purest form.

I will honor my innate power.

Endnotes

1. "heroine." *OxfordDictionaries.com*. 2015. http://www.oxforddictionaries.com/us/definition/american_english/heroine.

2. Warner, Judith. 2014. "Fact Sheet: The Women's Leadership Gap: Women's Leadership by the Numbers." *Center for American Progress*. https://www.americanprogress.org/issues/women/report/2014/03/07/85457/fact-sheet-the-womens-leadership-gap/.

3. "love." *OxfordDictionaries.com*. 2015. http://www.oxforddictionaries.com/us/definition/american_english/love.

4. "pain." *OxfordDictionaries.com*. 2015. http://www.oxforddictionaries.com/us/definition/american_english/pain.

5. "hope." *OxfordDictionaries.com*. 2015. http://www.oxforddictionaries.com/us/definition/american_english/hope.

6. "fear." *OxfordDictionaries.com*. 2015. http://www.oxforddictionaries.com/us/definition/american_english/fear.

7. "envy." *OxfordDictionaries.com*. 2015. http://www.oxforddictionaries.com/us/definition/american_english/envy.

8. "pride." *OxfordDictionaries.com*. 2015. http://www.oxforddictionaries.com/us/definition/american_english/pride.

9. "courage." *OxfordDictionaries.com*. 2015. http://www.oxforddictionaries.com/us/definition/american_english/courage.

10. "anger." *OxfordDictionaries.com*. 2015. http://www.oxforddictionaries.com/us/definition/american_english/anger.

11. "fatigue." *OxfordDictionaries.com*. 2015. http://www.oxforddictionaries.com/us/definition/american_english/fatigue.

12. "Heart Failure Statistics." 2015. *Emory Healthcare.org*. http://www.emoryhealthcare.org/heart-failure/learn-about-heart-failure/statistics.html.

13. "insecurity." *OxfordDictionaries.com*. 2015. http://www.oxforddictionaries.com/us/definition/american_english/insecurity.

14. "sadness." *OxfordDictionaries.com*. 2015. http://www.oxforddictionaries.com/us/definition/american_english/sadness.

15. "joy." *OxfordDictionaries.com*. 2015. http://www.oxforddictionaries.com/us/definition/american_english/joy.

16. "grace." *OxfordDictionaries.com*. 2015. http://www.oxforddictionaries.com/us/definition/american_english/grace.

17. "desire." *OxfordDictionaries.com*. 2015. http://www.oxforddictionaries.com/us/definition/american_english/desire.

18. "Newton's laws of motion." 2015. *Wikipedia.com*. http://www.emoryhealthcare.org/heart-failure/learn-about-heart-failure/statistics.html.

Lead Photographer

Charlton has captured breathtaking images for a variety of platforms including editorial, contemporary fashion, wedding and destination for over 15 years. As an international educator, Charlton has taught in 3 states and two countries including the United States and Saudi Arabia with his camera by his side at all times.

Charlton Hudnell, Lead Photographer

"Charlton has a discerning eye for beauty without limitations. His photography captures the emotion behind the image, a rare talent that is not often duplicated."

—Ardre Orie

Creative Director of Makeup Artistry

Sebastian, a highly acclaimed international makeup artist is often referred to as the "Guru of Transformation". Sebastian has spent over 20 years perfecting his craft for editorial and Special FX makeup and hair. Sebastian's coveted process for the transformation of the face is often referred to as the "Sebastian Experience". As a professional veteran, Sebastian has transformed models and professionals in all industries and will continue to be a moving force for the world to recognize.

Sebastian, Creative Director of Makeup Artistry

"Sebastian is the master of transformation. Many makeup artists transform people into someone else. Sebastian has mastered the art of transforming people into the absolute best versions of themselves. The human face is his canvas and he paints a beautiful portrait every time."

—Ardre Orie

About the Author

Through her work as an educator, mentor, entrepreneur, and author of A Heroine in Heels and Consciously Beautiful: I Am Enough, Ardre Orie has dedicated her life to empowering women. After teaching for six years and serving as an assistant principal for 4 years, she founded the Pink Wish Foundation, a 501(c)(3), to alleviate economic distress and self-destructive behaviors in girls ages 8–18, which has provided services to over 500 families in Florida and Georgia. Her cosmetic lines I Love Me and I Love Me Organics seek to inspire new generations of girls to live consciously beautiful lifestyles and take a stand against media messages that demean and devalue women. In June of 2013, Orie furthered that goal by launching I Love Me Magazine, an online and print publication devoted to spreading the message that true beauty comes from within.

Orie has since launched Consciously Beautiful TV to provide positive depictions of girls and women through media. In 2014, Orie made her directorial debut with her first play Lipstick Monologues, which provided a platform for women to articulate issues concerning love, life and self-esteem through the arts. Orie will release her first documentary entitled "I AM" that documents her journey to redefine beauty and the work of the Consciously Beautiful Movement. You can learn more about Ardre Orie and her mission at her website www.IAMardreorie.com.

Ardre Orie, Author

Connect with Ardre Orie:

Website: www.IAMardreorie.com
Facebook: www.facebook.com/IAMardreorie
Twitter: www.twitter.com/IAMardreorie
Instagram: www.instagram.com/IAMardreorie

www.ingramcontent.com/pod-product-compliance
Lightning Source LLC
Chambersburg PA
CBHW071925290426
44110CB00013B/1480